The Methuen Modern Plays series has a
modern playwriting. Since 1959, the s
exciting developments in modern drama, making the most significant
plays widely available in paperback.

Entertaining Mr Sloane

Entertaining Mr Sloane was first staged in 1964. Despite its success in
performance, and being hailed by Sir Terence Rattigan as 'the best
first play' he'd seen in 'thirty odd years', it was not until the London
production of *Loot* in 1966 – less than a year before Joe Orton's
untimely death – that theatre audiences and critics began to more fully
appreciate the originality of Orton's elegant, alarming and hilarious
writing. Introduced by John Lahr, the author of Orton's biography
Prick up Your Ears, *Entertaining Mr Sloane* is now established as an essential
part of the repertoire of the modern theatre.

'Unlike many scandals, both *Entertaining Mr Sloane* and its protagonist
reach their majority with impact undiminished . . . Mr Sloane has
moved with the times' *Financial Times*

Joe Orton was born in Leicester in 1933 and was battered to death by
his lover, Kenneth Halliwell, in August 1967. He left school at sixteen
and went to RADA two years later. He spent six months in prison for
defacing library books. His first play to be staged, *Entertaining Mr Sloane*,
won the London Critics' 'Variety' Award as the best play of 1964. *Loot*,
his second play to be staged, won the Evening Standard Drama Award
for the best play of 1966. *The Ruffian on the Stair* and *The Erpingham Camp*
were performed as a double bill at the Royal Court Theatre in June
1967 under the title *Crimes of Passion*. His television plays, *The Good and
Faithful Servant* and *Funeral Games*, were shown in 1967 and 1968. *What
the Butler Saw*, his last play, was staged in 1969, and won a 1970 'Obie'
Award for the best off-Broadway foreign play in New York. Both
Entertaining Mr Sloane and *Loot* have been filmed. Orton also wrote a
screenplay for the Beatles which was never filmed, but was
subsequently published as *Up Against It*. The novels, *Head to Toe*, *Between
Us Girls*, *The Boy Hairdresser* and *Lord Cucumber*, and the plays, *Fred and
Madge* and *The Visitors*, were published posthumously. *The Orton Diaries*
were published in 1986.

JOE ORTON

Entertaining Mr Sloane

introduced by JOHN LAHR

METHUEN

Methuen Modern Plays

3 5 7 9 10 8 6 4 2

First published by Hamish Hamilton 1964
Published in paperback by Penguin Books 1965
Published in 1973 by Eyre Methuen
Reissued by Methuen 1986

This edition, with new cover design, published in 2001 by
Methuen Publishing Limited
215 Vauxhall Bridge Road, London SW1V 1EJ

Copyright © 1964 by the Estate of Joe Orton

Methuen Publishing Limited Reg. No. 3543167

A CIP catalogue record for this book is available from the British Library

ISBN 0 413 41340 3

Printed and bound in Great Britain by
Cox & Wyman Ltd, Reading, Berkshire

Introduction

This was no ordinary Aunt Edna adding vindictive insult to injury
in the correspondence column of *Plays and Players*. It was Joe
Orton, under his frequent pseudonym, fanning the scandal of his
first produced play. The letter is typical of Orton's satiric flair: a
master of tone, a demolition expert of the disguises of decency. In
Orton, the wit and artifice of Oscar Wilde and the Restoration
dramatists were reincarnated on the English stage with a lethal twist.
All his plays dealt with violent death or the threat of it; and Orton, as
the major stage satirist of the '60's, knew about killing with laughter.
'To be destructive,' he wrote in his novel *Head to Toe*, 'Words
must be irrefutable . . . Print was less effective than the spoken
word because the blast was greater; eyes could ignore, slide past,
dangerous verbs or nouns. But if you could lock the enemy into a
room somewhere and fire the sentence at them you could get a sort
of seismic disturbance.'

Orton knew his enemy; and the relish he took in skewering it,
bred a kind of love. Kath's house is in the middle of a rubbish

dump. And the people in Orton's play live off the scraps of life. Their hunger, and how they idealize it, is what amuses Orton. 'In Germany,' he wrote to his American director, Alan Schneider. 'Eddie was the central pivot of the play. His stalking of the boy's arse was as funny and as wildly alarming as Kath's stalking of his cock. Unless this is so – you're in trouble.'

In following the ruthlessness of his characters' needs – their ignorance and unwitting violence – Orton was not being heartless, merely accurate. Sloane has killed one man when he walks into Kath's house looking for a room to let. By the time the play is over, he will have dispatched the second – Kath's father – only to be blackmailed into bed by Kath and her brother, Ed. Sloane is a survivor. A slick psychopath, he lives only to gratify his immediate needs. Sloane feels no guilt and his refusal to experience shame is what disturbs and amuses audiences. Sloane's egotism is rewarded, not punished. Orton wrote to Alan Schneider:

I don't know what you mean about the Eddie-Sloane relationship. Quite clear. Sloane knows Eddie wants him. He has absolutely no qualms about surrendering his body. None. He's done it many, many times. Sloane is no virgin. He's been in bed with men and women in the past. But he isn't going to give in until he has to. And while he can get away with . . . riding around in cars, just fucking Kath a couple of times a week, getting paid a good salary, why should he give up the trump card. Eddie, naturally, doesn't know how amoral Sloane is. He imagines that he has a virgin on his hands. He thinks he can get Sloane. Sure he can. But it may take a bit of time – cause Sloane is such a nice kid. Where's the problem?

Sloane, and the menagerie of hilarious egomaniacs in Orton's two other major plays *Loot* and *What the Butler Saw*, never admit or understand how much their sensibility has been shaped by the society. But Orton understands. He was the first playwright to dramatize the psychopathic style of the '60's – that restless, ruthless, single-minded pursuit of satisfaction – transformed by drugs and rock music into myth. In his plays, the characters are always numb to their death-dealing. Orton delights in playing off this fact against the dramatic situation. Kath's father lies bludgeoned upstairs, while downstairs, the triangle tries to sort things out.

SLOANE. Leave her to me.

KATH. Don't attempt to threaten me.

ED. There's no suggestion of threats.

KATH. What's he doing, then?

ED. Let her alone, boy.

(ED *lays a hand on* SLOANE'S *shoulder, tries to pull him away from* KATH. SLOANE *turns, shoves* ED *from him*.)

Did you hear what I said? Keep out of it!

ED. Don't be violent. No violence at any cost. (SLOANE *gets* KATH *into a corner; struggles with her*.) What's this exhibition for? This is gratuitous violence . . .

When *Entertaining Mr Sloane* opened in May 1964, it was clear that Orton's voice was an exciting and unusual one. Sir Terence Rattigan proclaimed it 'the best first play' he'd seen in 'thirty odd years'. On the other hand, when the play transferred to the West End, impresario Emile Littler and Peter Cadbury, chairman of London's largest ticket bureau, joined forces in an attack hotly reported in the press, damning *Entertaining Mr Sloane* as a dirty highbrow play which should never have been allowed in the West End. Even when *Entertaining Mr Sloane* was chosen to be published in Penguin's *New English Dramatists 8*, John Russell Taylor, writing the introduction, would only grudgingly concede Orton's talent. 'Living theatre needs the good commercial dramatist as much as the original artist.' While Orton delighted in the public brouhaha over his play, he was furious with such critical stupidity. 'Are they different, then?' he asked, quoting John Russell Taylor's distinction between commercial success and art to his agent and asking to withdraw the play from the volume. '*Hamlet* was written by a commercial dramatist. So were *Volpone* and *The School for Scandal* and *The Importance of Being Earnest* and *The Cherry Orchard* and *Our Betters*. Two ex-commercial successes of the last thirty years are about to be revived by our non-commercial theatre: *A Cuckoo in the Nest* and *Hay Fever* . . . I've no ambition to bolster up the commercial theatre, but if my plays go on in the West End I don't expect this to be used as a sneer by people who judge artistic success by commercial failure. There is no intrinsic merit in a flop.'

Orton, who studied to be an actor at RADA and graduated in 1953, left the stage almost immediately, devoting himself to a decade of literary apprenticeship. In that time, he read widely and experimented in many genres. He understood the solid foundation of his talent. 'I'd attempted to do novels before *Sloane*,' Orton told the BBC in 1964. 'But I'd always been interested in the theatre, and you see I can write dialogue and language, dialogue, it's the same thing. And unless you're Ivy Compton Burnett, you can't write a complete novel with just dialogue, so it's obvious to use the play form. As I was interested in the theatre, it was natural that I should write a play.'

Orton's dialogue is a collage of the popular culture. It assimilates advertising jargon, the idioms of the popular press, the stilted lusciousness of Grade-B movies. Like the characters in his plays, a poetry is forged from words debased and thrown-away by the culture. His characters do not speak in the refined, heroic language of Osborne and Arden. Orton does something much more elusive and difficult. He adds his own brand of irony to the colloquial. Fantasy finds its way into the sentences of his characters, and their words stand out like banners flagging their dream to the audience if not themselves. Kath's confidences gloss her slovenliness:

KATH. I married out of school. I surprised everyone by the sudden-
ness of it. (*Pause.*) Does that sound as if I had to get married.
SLOANE. I'm broadminded.
KATH. I should've known better. You won't breathe a word?
SLOANE. You can trust me.
KATH. My brother would be upset if he knew I told you. (*Pause.*)
Nobody knows around here. The people in the nursing home
imagined I *was* somebody. I didn't disillusion them.

Kath exudes a sense of emotional starvation. She eyes Sloane with the voluptuous anticipation of a cat watching a canary. She con-fesses, 'You have the air of lost wealth.' The sentence catches us by surprise. Its romantic refinement is just wrong, and therefore funny, in context. This is Orton's verbal trademark which he would take to extremes in his later plays. No contemporary playwright could unleash such devastating humour in a line. For instance:

1. *The Erpingham Camp :* 'With madness as with vomit, it is the passer-by who receives the inconvenience."

2. *What the Butler Saw :* 'You can't be a rationalist in an irrational world. It isn't rational.'

3. *Loot :* 'Go ahead. Ask me to marry you. I've no intention of refusing. On your knees. I'm a great believer in traditional positions.'

'I think you should use the language of your age, and use every bit of it, not just a little bit,' Orton told the BBC. 'They always go on about poetic drama and they think that you have to sort of go off into some high flown fantasy, but it isn't poetic drama, it's everything, it's the language in use at the time. I have to be very careful in the way that I write, not to let it become sort of a mannerism, it could very easily become a mannerism.'

Orton's admitted strength in *Entertaining Mr Sloane* also belies a theatrical limitation. *Entertaining Mr Sloane* is Orton's most naturalistic work, and the piece does not use the stage with full playfulness – a fact Orton recognized. *Loot* and *What the Butler Saw* work more boldly with theatrical artifice. Orton considered them an advance, a development in which his dazzling capacity to manipulate words was matched with an equally startling talent for constructing hilarious stage images. In *Entertaining Mr Sloane,* Orton was toying with farce. Kath loses her teeth and is grovelling on all fours at the play's tensest moment. The cut and thrust rhythm of the play's third act dialogue has a potential for mayhem that never gets beyond the vaudeville of language to movement.

SLOANE. Is it going to be O.K.?

ED. Well . . . perhaps.

SLOANE. I'll be grateful.

ED. Will you?

SLOANE. Eternally.

ED. Not eternally, boy. Just a few years.

And finally, it is as a farceur that Orton's reputation continues to grow. He succeeded in taking a frivolous form and turning it to resonant ends. Conscious of the theatre's literary heritage, his plays extend the style and savagery of Restoration comedy into twentieth century life. With farce, his characters move at a momentum which augurs their disintegration. They defy – in both senses of the word – gravity. Orton's farces carried out Nietzsche's commandment in *Thus Spake Zarathustra.* 'And when I beheld my devil, I found him serious, thorough, profound, solemn; it was the Spirit of Gravity, through him all things are ruined. One does not kill by anger but by laughter. Come let us kill the Spirit of Gravity.'

Orton waged his war with a clear understanding of his goals. In the three years before his death in August 1967 at the age of 34, his confidence and technique grew. He offered an audience grotesques which, like the gargoyles on a medieval cathedral, forced the viewer to imagine Hell and redefine Heaven. To him, nothing was sacred; but the fury of his attack, its peculiar combination of joy and horror, was not without a broader spiritual motive. Orton wanted to shock the society and also to purify it. On stage, his characters are performing animals. And, once the beast in every man is faced, then tolerance can more easily replace righteousness.

Orton was battered to death by the man to whom *Entertaining Mr Sloane* is dedicated, a victim of the very possessiveness the play satirizes. At the time, the death was more famous than the plays. But the years and our violent history have reversed the situation. Critics and audiences are now beginning to recognize Orton's staying power. His style is too unique, his humour too side-splitting, his stage metaphors too accurate for him to be relegated to history's rubbish heap. In showing us how we destroy ourselves, Orton's plays are themselves a survival tactic. He makes us laugh to make us learn. There is a salvation in that.

JOHN LAHR

ENTERTAINING MR SLOANE

To Kenneth Halliwell

Entertaining Mr Sloane was first presented in London at the New Arts Theatre on 6 May 1964 by Michael Codron Ltd and at Wyndhams Theatre on 29 June 1964 by Michael Codron and Albery, with the following cast:

KATH	Madge Ryan
SLOANE	Dudley Sutton
KEMP	Charles Lamb
ED	Peter Vaughan

Directed by Patrick Dromgoole
Designed by Timothy O'Brien
Costumes supervised by Tazeena Firth

ACT ONE

A room. Evening.

> KATH *enters followed by* SLOANE.

KATH. This is my lounge.

SLOANE. Would I be able to use this room? Is it included?

KATH. Oh, yes. (*Pause.*) You mustn't imagine it's always like this. You ought to have rung up or something. And then I'd've been prepared.

SLOANE. The bedroom was perfect.

KATH. I never showed you the toilet.

SLOANE. I'm sure it will be satisfactory. (*Walks around the room examining the furniture. Stops by the window.*)

KATH. I should change them curtains. Those are our winter ones. The summer ones are more of a chintz. (*Laughs.*) The walls need re-doing. The Dadda has trouble with his eyes. I can't ask him to do any work involving ladders. It stands to reason.

> *Pause.*

SLOANE. I can't give you a decision right away.

KATH. I don't want to rush you. (*Pause.*) What do you think? I'd be happy to have you.

> *Silence.*

SLOANE. Are you married?

KATH (*pause*). I was. I had a boy . . . killed in very sad circumstances. It broke my heart at the time. I got over it though. You do, don't you?

> *Pause.*

SLOANE. A son?

KATH. Yes.

SLOANE. You don't look old enough.

Pause.

KATH. I don't let myself go like some of them you may have noticed. I'm just over . . . As a matter of fact I'm forty-one.

Pause.

SLOANE (*briskly*). I'll take the room.

KATH. Will you?

SLOANE. I'll bring my things over tonight. It'll be a change from my previous.

KATH. Was it bad?

SLOANE. Bad?

KATH. As bad as that?

SLOANE. You've no idea.

KATH. I don't suppose I have. I've led a sheltered life.

SLOANE. Have you been a widow long?

KATH. Yes a long time. My husband was a mere boy. (*With a half-laugh*).) That sounds awful doesn't it?

SLOANE. Not at all.

KATH. I married out of school. I surprised everyone by the suddenness of it. (*Pause.*) Does that sound as if I had to get married?

SLOANE. I'm broadminded.

KATH. I should've known better. You won't breathe a word?

SLOANE. You can trust me.

KATH. My brother would be upset if he knew I told you. (*Pause.*) Nobody knows around here. The people in the nursing home imagined I *was* somebody. I didn't disillusion them.

SLOANE. You were never married then?

KATH. No.

SLOANE. What about – I hope you don't think I'm prying?

KATH. I wouldn't for a minute. What about –?

SLOANE. . . . the father?

KATH (*pause*). We always planned to marry. But there were difficulties. I was very young and he was even younger. I don't believe we would have been allowed.

SLOANE. What happened to the baby?

KATH. Adopted.

SLOANE. By whom?

KATH. That I could not say. My brother arranged it.

SLOANE. What about the kid's father?

KATH. He couldn't do anything.

SLOANE. Why not?

KATH. His family objected. They were very nice but he had a duty you see. (*Pause.*) As I say, if it'd been left to him I'd be his widow today. (*Pause.*) I had a last letter. I'll show you some time. (*Silence.*) D'you like flock or foam rubber in your pillow?

SLOANE. Foam rubber.

KATH. You need a bit of luxury, don't you? I bought the Dadda one but he can't stand them.

SLOANE. I can.

KATH. You'll live with us then as one of the family?

SLOANE. I never had no family of my own.

KATH. Didn't you?

SLOANE. No. I was brought up in an orphanage.

KATH. You have the air of lost wealth.

SLOANE. That's remarkable. My parents, I believe, *were* extremely wealthy people.

KATH. Did Dr Barnardo give you a bad time?

SLOANE. No. It was the lack of privacy I found most trying.

Pause.

And the lack of real love.

KATH. Did you never know your mamma?

SLOANE. Yes.

KATH. When did they die?

SLOANE. I was eight. (*Pause.*) They passed away together.

KATH. How shocking.

SLOANE. I've an idea that they had a suicide pact. Couldn't prove it of course.

KATH. Of course not. (*Pause.*) With a nice lad like you to take care of you'd think they'd've postponed it. (*Pause.*) Criminals, were they?

SLOANE. From what I remember they was respected. You know, H.P. debts. Bridge. A little light gardening. The usual activities of a cultured community. (*Silence.*) I respect their memory.

KATH. Do you? How nice.

SLOANE. Every year I pay a visit to their grave. I take sandwiches. Make a day of it. (*Pause.*) The graveyard is situated in pleasant surroundings so it's no hardship. (*Pause.*) Tomb an' all.

KATH. Marble? (*Pause.*) Is there an inscription?

SLOANE. Perhaps you'd come with me this trip?

KATH. We'll see.

SLOANE. I go in the autumn because I clean the leaves off the monument. As a tribute.

KATH. Yes.

SLOANE. That's the main task I set myself.

KATH. Any relations?

SLOANE. None.

KATH. Poor boy. Alone in the world. Like me.

SLOANE. You're not alone.

KATH. I am. (*Pause.*) Almost alone. (*Pause.*) If I'd been allowed to keep my boy I'd not be. (*Pause.*) You're almost the same age as he would be. You've got the same refinement.

SLOANE (*slowly*). I need . . . understanding.

KATH. You do, don't you? Here let me take your coat. (*Helps him off with his coat.*) You've got a delicate skin. (*Touches his neck. His cheek.*)

He shudders a little. Pause.

KATH (*kisses his cheek*). Just a motherly kiss. A real mother's kiss. (*Silence. Lifts his arms and folds them about her.*) You'll find me very sentimental. I upset easy. (*His arms are holding her.*) When

I hear of . . . tragedies happening to perfect strangers. There are so many ruined lives. (*Puts her head on his shoulder*.) You must treat me gently when I'm in one of my moods.

Silence.

SLOANE. (*clearing his throat*). How much are you charging? I mean – I've got to know.

He drops his arms. She moves away.

KATH. We'll come to some arrangement. A cup of tea?

SLOANE. Yes I don't mind.

KATH. I'll get you one.

SLOANE. Can I have a bath?

KATH. Now?

SLOANE. Later would do.

KATH. You must do as you think fit.

A door slams. KEMP's *voice is heard off.*

KEMP. You there?

KATH (*calls*). I'm in here. Don't stand about. Sit down. Go on. We don't charge.

SLOANE *sits on the settee.*

That's a lovely shade of blue on your woolly. I'll fetch you one down later that I knitted for my brother.

KEMP *enters.*

(*loudly*). We have a visitor, Dadda.

KEMP. Eh?

KATH. A visitor.

KEMP (*stares, lifts his glasses and stares again*). Oh . . . It's Eddie?

KATH. You are the limit. You show me up no end. It isn't Ed. (*Pause.*) You behave like a sick child. I'm just about tired of it. Afraid to have a guest or a friend in the house. You put them off, Dadda. Let him shake your hand. Go on.

KEMP *shakes* SLOANE's *hand.*

KEMP. What's he want, then?

KATH. Mr Sloane is going to stay with us.

KEMP. Stay with us?

KATH. That's what I said.

KEMP. He can't. We've no room.

KATH. Make an effort will you? What will the gentleman think?
He'll think you're a rude old man. (*Exchanges looks with*
SLOANE.) I'm going to have to apologize for your boorish
attitude. Do you feel embarrassed, Mr Sloane?

SLOANE. It's all right.

KATH. No, it isn't. (*To* KEMP) Pull yourself together! (*Silence.*)
Can I trust you to behave yourself while I get something to eat?

KEMP *does not answer.*

Entertain Mr Sloane now. Give him the benefit of your
experience. (*Pause.*) You want to learn manners. That's what
you want. (*Picks up a basket of provisions from the floor.*) I'm a
good mind to give you no tea. (*To* SLOANE) I'd not care to
wonder what you must think of us. (*Takes a packet of crumpets
from the basket. Hands it to* KEMP.) Here, toast these. Give
yourself something to do. (*Exits.*)

KEMP *goes to fire. Begins to toast crumpets.*

SLOANE. Haven't we met before?

KEMP. Not to my knowledge.

SLOANE. Your face is familiar. Have I seen your photo in the
paper? In connexion with some event?

KEMP. No.

SLOANE. Do you pop into the pub at the end of the road?

KEMP. I don't drink.

SLOANE. Are you a churchgoer?

KEMP. Not at the moment. I used to be. In the old days I'd
knock up the Vicar at all hours. But then I lost touch.

SLOANE. I've seen you somewhere. I very rarely forget a face.

KEMP. Y've got me confused with another person.

SLOANE. Perhaps.

KEMP. Forget it, son. I'm not seen about much.

SLOANE. (*Pause*). You don't resent my being in the house, do you?

KEMP. Not at all.

SLOANE. I thought you did. Just now.

KEMP. No.

SLOANE. This seems a nice place. Friendly atmosphere. (*Pause.*) How many children have you?

KEMP. Two.

SLOANE. Is your daughter married?

KEMP. She was. Had a terrible time. Kiddy died.

SLOANE. You have a son, don't you?

KEMP. Yes, but we're not on speaking terms.

SLOANE. How long is it?

KEMP. Twenty years.

SLOANE. 'Strewth!

KEMP. You perhaps find that hard to believe?

SLOANE. I do actually. Not speaking for twenty years? That's coming it a bit strong.

KEMP. I may have exchanged a few words.

SLOANE. I can believe that.

KEMP. He was a good boy. Played some amazing games as a youth. Won every goal at football one season. Sport mad, he was. (*Pause.*) Then one day, shortly after his seventeenth birthday, I had cause to return home unexpected and found him committing some kind of felony in the bedroom.

SLOANE. Is that straight?

KEMP. I could never forgive him.

SLOANE. A puritan, are you?

KEMP. Yes.

SLOANE. That kind of thing happens often, I believe. For myself, I usually lock the door.

KEMP. I'd removed the lock.

SLOANE. Anticipating some such tendencies on his part?

KEMP. I'd done it as a precautionary measure.

SLOANE. There are fascinating possibilities in this situation. I'd get it down on paper if I were you. (*Goes to the window.*)

KEMP. Admiring the view?

SLOANE. A perfect skyline you've got here. Lord Snowdon would give you something for a shot of that. Stunning it is. Stunning. Was this house a speculation?

KEMP. Not exactly.

SLOANE. Who built it then? Was he a mad financier? The bloke who conceived the idea of building a house in the midst of a rubbish dump?

KEMP. It was intended to be the first of a row.

SLOANE. Go on. What happened?

KEMP. They gave up.

SLOANE. Lost interest?

KEMP. There were financial restrictions.

SLOANE. What a way to carry on!

KEMP. We've tried putting in complaints, but it's no good. Look at it out there. An eyesore. You may admire it. I don't. A woman came all the way from Woolwich yesterday. A special trip she made in order to dump a bedstead. I told her, what do you want to saddle us with your filthy mess for? Came over in a shooting-brake. She was an old woman. Had her daughter with her. Fouling the countryside with their litter.

SLOANE. What you want is someone with pull on the council.

KEMP. If my boss were here I'd go to him.

SLOANE. Wealthy, was he?

KEMP. He had holdings in some trust. He didn't go into details with me.

SLOANE. How old was he?

KEMP. Forty.

SLOANE. Early middle-age?

KEMP. Yes.

SLOANE. Dead, is he?

KEMP. Yes.

SLOANE. Did he die for his country?

KEMP. No. He was murdered. On the unsolved crimes list, he is.

SLOANE. A murderer not brought to justice. That's a sobering thought. (*Pause.*) Why can't they find the murderer? Didn't they advertise?

KEMP. Yes. They took a piece in the local paper.

SLOANE. How long ago was all this?

KEMP. Two years.

SLOANE. Do they have any clue to the murderer's identity?

KEMP. He was a young man with very smooth skin.

SLOANE (*pause*). Was your boss a small man?

KEMP. Yes. Wavy hair. Wore a tweed tie.

SLOANE. What was his profession?

KEMP. He was a photographer. Specialized in views of the river.

SLOANE. You were employed in his service?

KEMP. Yes. As a general handyman. (*Pause.*) We gave the murderer a lift on the night of the crime.

SLOANE (*pause*). You saw him then?

KEMP. Yes.

SLOANE. Why didn't you go to the police?

KEMP. I can't get involved in that type of case. I might get my name in the papers.

SLOANE. I see your point of view. (*Pause.*) They won't find the killer now.

KEMP. I should very much doubt it.

SLOANE. No, the scent's gone cold.

He watches KEMP *in silence.*

Have you ever toasted a crumpet before?

KEMP. Yes.

SLOANE. I thought it was your first time from the way you're messing that about.

KEMP *does not reply.*

KEMP (*pause*). Come here.

SLOANE. Why?

KEMP. I want to look at you.

SLOANE. What for?

KEMP. I think we have met before.

SLOANE. No, Pop. I'm convinced we haven't. I must have been getting you mixed up with a man called Fergusson. He had the same kind of way with him. Trustworthy.

KEMP. You think that?

SLOANE. Yes (*Laughs.*)

KEMP (*pause*). Fetch me a plate, will you?

SLOANE. Where from?

KEMP. The dresser. Back there.

> SLOANE *goes to the dresser. Fetches a plate. Comes to* KEMP, *bends down to give him the plate.* KEMP *seizes* SLOANE'S *arm, pulls him towards him.*

SLOANE. What's this!

KEMP. We have met before! I knew we had.

SLOANE. I've never met you.

KEMP. On my life. I remember.

SLOANE. Your eyes aren't good.

KEMP. I could still identify you.

SLOANE (*pause*). Identify me?

KEMP. If it was necessary.

SLOANE. How could it be necessary?

KEMP. It might be.

SLOANE. Do lay off, Pop. You couldn't identify a herring on a plate!

KEMP. Don't speak to me like that, sonny. You'll find yourself in trouble.

SLOANE. Go on, you superannuated old prat!

KEMP. I'll have somebody to you. See if I don't.

> SLOANE *turns away.*

SLOANE. Why don't you shut your mouth and give your arse a chance?

KEMP *lunges at* SLOANE *with the toasting fork.* SLOANE *gives a squeal of pain.*

SLOANE. Oh, you bleeding maniac! My leg. My leg.

KEMP. You provoked me!

SLOANE (*sinks into an armchair*). I'll be in a wheelchair for life. (*Examines his leg.*) Oh, you cow. I'm covered in blood! Call somebody!

KEMP (*goes to the door, shouting*). Kathy! Kathy!

KATH. (*runs on, drying her hands on her apron, sees* SLOANE, *screams*). What've you done?

KEMP. It wasn't intentional. (*Comes forward.*)

KATH (*shoos him away*). Is there pain?

SLOANE. I can't move.

KATH. Are you hurt bad?

SLOANE. He's got an artery. I must be losing pints. Oh, Christ!

KATH. Come on. You'll be better on the settee. (*He allows her to guide him over. She settles him.*) What happened? Did he attack you? He's never shown signs before.

KEMP. I thought he was further off. I can't judge distances.

KATH. Let Mr Sloane speak for himself.

SLOANE. He ought to be in Colney Hatch. He's a slate off. Throwing things about.

KATH. Throw them, did he?

SLOANE. I don't know what he did.

KATH. I'm ashamed of you, Dadda. Really ashamed. I think you behave very badly. Lie down, Mr Sloane. (*To* KEMP.) Go and get the Dettol and some water. Make yourself useful.

 KEMP *shuffles off.*

I never realized he was antagonistic to you, Mr Sloane. Perhaps he's jealous. We were getting on so well. (*Pause.*) Is it hurting you?

SLOANE. Can you get a bandage?

KATH. I will. (*Goes to the sideboard and rummages in a drawer. Rummages again. Repeat. Second drawer. Takes out and places on top of the sideboard a Boots folder containing snapshots and negatives, a reel of cotton, a piece of unfinished knitting, a tattered knitting pattern, a broken china figure, a magazine, a doorknob and several pieces of silk.)*

SLOANE (*calling impatiently*). There's blood running on your settee. You'll have a stain, I can see it coming.

KATH (*runs back with a piece of silk. Lifts his leg. Spreads the silk under the bloody patch*). This'll do. It's a piece of material my brother brought back. It's good stuff. I was intending to make a blouse but there's not enough.

SLOANE. What's he doing with that Dettol? Is he gone to Swansea for it?

KATH (*shouting*). What are you doing, Dadda? He gets that thick. (*Goes to sideboard.*)

KEMP *enters with a bottle of Dettol.*

KATH (*takes it from him*). You done enough damage for one day. Make yourself scarce.

He shuffles off.

And don't be eating anything out there. (*Pushes past him. Returns with a saucepan full of water. After hunting in sideboard finds a torn towel. Comes to* SLOANE. *Kneels.*) What a lovely pair of shoes you got. (*Unlacing his shoes she takes them off and places them under the settee.*)

SLOANE. I think I'm going to spew.

KATH *hastily holds the saucepan under him.*

No. I'll be all right.

KATH. I wonder, Mr Sloane, if you'd take your trousers off? I hope you don't think there's anything behind the request. (*Looks at him.*)

He unloosens his belt.

I expect you guessed as much before I asked. If you'll lift up I'll pull them off. (*Tugs the trousers free.*)

SLOANE *tucks the tail of his shirt between his legs.*

KATH. That's right. (*Pause.*) Where is it then?

SLOANE. Here. (*Pointing and lifting his leg.*)

KATH. He attacked you from behind? If you ask me it's only a deep scratch. (*Pause.*) I don't think we'll require outside assistance. (*Pause.*) Don't be embarrassed, Mr Sloane. I'd the upbringing a nun would envy and that's the truth. Until I was fifteen I was more familiar with Africa than my own body. That's why I'm so pliable. (*Applies Dettol.*)

SLOANE. Ouch!

KATH. Just the thing for the germs. (*Pause.*) You've a skin on you like a princess. Better than on those tarts you see dancing about on the telly. I like a lad with a smooth body. (*Stops dabbing his leg. Takes up the bandage. Rises. Fetches a pair of scissors. Cuts bandage. Ties it round* SLOANE'*s leg.*) Isn't it strange that the hairs on your legs should be dark?

SLOANE. Eh?

KATH. Attractive, though.

SLOANE. Dark?

KATH. Yes. You being a blond.

SLOANE. Oh, yes.

KATH. Nature's a funny thing.

Ring on the doorbell.

SLOANE. Who's that?

KATH. Keep your voice down. (*Pause.*) It's probably her from the shops. I'll not answer it. She's only got one subject for talk.

SLOANE. She'll hear.

KATH. Not if you keep your voice down.

Prolonged ringing.

SLOANE. What about Pop?

KATH. He won't answer. I don't want her in here. She tells everybody her business. And if she found me in this predicament she'd think all kinds of things. (*Pause.*) Her daughter's involved in a court case at the moment. Tells every detail. The details are endless. I suffer as she recounts. Oh, Mr Sloane, if only I'd been born without ears. (*Silence. Finishes tying the bandage and squats on her haunches looking up at him. Pause.*) Is that bandage too tight?

SLOANE. No.

KATH. I wouldn't want to restrict your circulation.

SLOANE. It's O.K.

She picks up his trousers.

KATH. I'll sponge these, and there's a nick in the material. I'll fix it. (*Puts Dettol, bandage, etc, into the sideboard.*) This drawer is my medicine cabinet, dear. If you wants an occasional aspirin help yourself. (*She comes back.*)

He lies full length; she smiles. Silence.

KATH (*confidentially*). I've been doing my washing today and I haven't a stitch on ... except my shoes ... I'm in the rude under this dress. I tell you because you're bound to have noticed ...

Silence. SLOANE *attempts to reach his trouser pocket.*

Don't move, dear. Not yet. Give the blood time to steady itself.

SLOANE *takes the nylon stocking from between cushions of settee.*

I wondered where I'd left it.

SLOANE. Is it yours?

KATH. Yes. You'll notice the length? I've got long legs. Long, elegant legs. (*Kicks out her leg.*) I could give one or two of them a surprise. (*Pause.*) My look is quite different when I'm in private. (*Leans over him.*) You can't see through this dress can you? I been worried for fear of embarrassing you.

SLOANE *lifts his hand and touches the point where he judges her nipple to be.*

KATH (*leaps back*). Mr Sloane – don't betray your trust.

SLOANE. I just thought –

KATH. I know what you thought. You wanted to see if my titties were all my own. You're all the same. (*Smirks.*) I must be careful of you. Have me naked on the floor if I give you a chance. If my brother was to know . . . (*Pause.*) . . . he's such a possessive man. (*Silence. Stands up.*) Would you like to go to bed?

SLOANE. It's early.

KATH. You need rest. You've had a shock. (*Pause.*) I'll bring your supper to your room.

SLOANE. What about my case?

KATH. The Dadda will fetch it. (*Pause.*) Can you get up the stairs on your own?

SLOANE. Mmmm.

KATH (*motions him back. Stands in front of him*). Just a minute. (*Calls*). Dadda! (*Pause.*) Dadda!

> KEMP *appears in the doorway.*

KEMP. What?

KATH. Turn your face away. Mr Sloane is passing. He has no trousers on. (*Quietly to Sloane.*) You know the room?

SLOANE. Yes.

> *Silence.* SLOANE *exits.*

KATH (*calling after him*). Have a bath if you want to, dear. Treat the conveniences as if they were your own. (*Turns to* KEMP.) I want an explanation.

KEMP. Yes. Kathy . . .

KATH. Don't Kathy me.

KEMP. But he upset me.

KATH. Upset you? A grown man?

KEMP. I've seen him before.

KATH. You've seen the milkman before. That's no cause to throw the shears at him.

KEMP. I didn't throw them.

KATH. Oh? I heard different. (*Picks up her handbag and takes out money.*) Go and fetch his case. It'll be about five pence on the bus.

(*Presses the money into his hand.*) The address is 39 St Hilary's Crescent.

KEMP. Where's that?

KATH (*losing her temper*). By the Co-op! Behave yourself.

KEMP. A teetotal club on the corner is there?

KATH. That's the one. Only it is closed. (*Pause.*) Can you find it?

KEMP. I expect so.

>   *There is a noise of tapping.*

KATH (*goes to the window. Over her shoulder*). It's Eddie.

KEMP. What's that?

KATH (*speaking to someone outside*). Why don't you come round the right way?

ED (*outside the window*). I rung the bell but you was out.

KATH. Are you coming in?

ED. I'll be round. (*Closes the window.*)

KATH. It's Eddie.

KEMP. I'm not going to talk to him!

KATH. I don't expect he wants you to.

KEMP. He knows I'm in always on Friday. (*Pause.*) I'm signing nothing you can tell him that.

KATH. Tell him what?

KEMP. That I'm not signing nothing.

ED (*entering*). Is he still on? What's the matter with you?

>   KEMP *does not reply.*

Always on about something.

KEMP. I'm not speaking to him.

ED (*patiently*). Go on, get out of it afore I kicks you out. Make me bad you do. With your silly, childish ways.

>   KEMP *does not reply.*

KATH. Do what I told you, Dadda. Try not to lose yourself. Follow the railings. Then ask somebody.

> KEMP *exits.*
>
> KATH *dips towel in saucepan, begins to sponge bloody patch on settee.*

ED (*watches her. Takes a drag of his cigarette*). What's this I heard about you?

KATH. What?

ED. Listening are you?

KATH. Yes, Eddie, I'm listening.

ED. You've got a kid staying here.

KATH. No . . .

ED. Don't lie to me.

KATH. He's a guest. He's not a lodger.

ED. Who told you to take in lodgers?

> *Pause.*

KATH. I needed a bit extra.

ED. I'll give you the money.

KATH. I'm taking Dadda away next year.

> *Pause.*

ED. I don't want men hanging around.

KATH. He's a nice young man.

ED. You know what these fellows are – young men with no fixed abode.

KATH. No.

ED. You know what they say about landladies?

KATH. No, Eddie.

ED. They say they'd sleep with a broom handle in trousers, that's what they say.

KATH (*uneasy*). I'm not like that.

ED. You're good-natured though. They mistake it.

KATH. This young man is quite respectable.

ED. You've got to realize my position. I can't have my sister keeping a common kip. Some of my associates are men of distinction. They think nothing of tipping a fiver. That sort of person. If they realized how my family carry on I'd be banned from the best places. (*Pause.*) And another thing . . . you don't want them talking about you. An' I can't guarantee my influence will keep them quiet. Nosy neighbours and scandal. Oh, my word, the looks you'll get. (*Pause.*) How old is he?

KATH. He's young.

ED. These fellows sleep with their landladies automatic. Has he made suggestions? Suggested you bring him supper in bed?

KATH. No.

ED. That's what they do. Then they take advantage.

KATH. Mr Sloane is superior to that.

ED. Where did you find him?

KATH. In the library.

ED. Picked him up, did you?

KATH. He was having trouble. With his rent. (*Pause.*) His landlady was unscrupulous.

ED. How long have you been going with him?

KATH. He's a good boy.

    ED *sees trousers, picks them up.*

KATH. It was an accident.

ED. Had the trousers off him already I see. (*Balls his fist and punches her upper arm gently.*) Don't let me down, darlin'. (*Pause.*) Where is he?

KATH. Upstairs.

ED. You fetch him.

KATH. He hurt his leg.

ED. I want to see him.

KATH. He's resting. (*Pause.*) Ed, you won't tell him to go?

ED (*brushing her aside*). Go and fetch him.

KATH. I'm not misbehaving. Ed, if you send him away I shall cry.

ED (*raising his voice*). Let's have less of it. I'll decide.

She exits.

ED (*calls after her*). Tell him to put his trousers on. (*Picks up the trousers and flings them after her.*) Cantering around the house with a bare bum. Good job I come when I did. (*Pause.*) Can't leave you alone for five minutes.

KATH (*off*). Mr Sloane! Would you step down here for a minute? My brother would like to meet you. (*Re-enters.*) He's trustworthy. Visits his parents once a month. Asked me to go with him. You couldn't object to a visit to a graveyard? The sight of the tombs would deter any looseness. (*Sniffs. Shrugs. Picks through the junk on the sideboard, finds a sweet and puts it in her mouth.*) He hasn't any mamma of his own. I'm to be his mamma. He's an orphan. Eddie, he wouldn't do wrong. Please don't send him away.

ED. It'd crease me if you misbehaved again. I got responsibilities.

KATH. Let him stay.

ED. Kid like that. Know what they'll say, don't you?

Pause.

KATH. He's cultured, Ed. He's informed.

ED *turns and lights another cigarette from the butt of the one he is smoking. Opens the window. Throws the butt out.* SLOANE *enters.*

KATH. This is my brother, Mr Sloane. He expressed a desire to meet you.

ED (*turns, faces* SLOANE). I . . . my sister was telling me about you.

Pause.

My sister was telling me about you being an orphan, Mr Sloane.

SLOANE (*smiling*). Oh, yes?

ED. Must be a rotten life for a kid. You look well on it though.

SLOANE. Yes.

ED. I could never get used to sleeping in cubicles. Was it a mixed home?

SLOANE. Just boys.

ED. Ideal. How many to a room?

SLOANE. Eight.

ED. Really? Same age were they? Or older?

SLOANE. The ages varied by a year or two.

ED. Oh well, you had compensations then. Keep you out of mischief, eh? (*Laughs.*) Well your childhood wasn't unhappy?

SLOANE. No.

ED. Sounds as though it was a happy atmosphere. (*Pause.*) Got anything to do, Kath?

KATH. No.

ED. No beds to make?

KATH. I made them this morning.

ED. Maybe you forgot to change the pillowslips?

KATH (*going*). Eddie don't let me be upset will you? (*Exits.*)

ED. I must apologize for her behaviour. She's not in the best of health.

SLOANE. She seems all right.

ED. You can't always go on appearances. She's . . . well I wouldn't say unbalanced. No, that'd be going too far. She suffers from migraine. That's why it'd be best if you declined her offer of a room.

SLOANE. I see.

ED. When are you going?

SLOANE. But I like it here.

ED. I dare say you do. The fact is my sister's taking on too many responsibilities. She's a charming woman as a rule. Charming. I've no hesitation in saying that. Lost her husband. And her little kid. Tell you did she?

SLOANE. She mentioned it.

ED (*wary*). What did she say?

SLOANE. Said she married young.

ED. She married a mate of mine – a valiant man – we were together in Africa.

SLOANE. In the army?

ED. You're interested in the army, eh? Soldiers, garrison towns, etc. Does that interest you?

SLOANE. Yes.

ED. Good, excellent. How old are you?

SLOANE. Twenty.

ED. Married?

SLOANE. No.

ED (*laughs*). Wise man, eh? Wise man. (*Pause.*) Girl friends?

SLOANE. No.

ED. No. You're a librarian?

SLOANE. No.

ED. I thought she said –

SLOANE. I help out at Len's . . . the tobacconist. Give him a hand. I'm not employed there.

ED. I was told you were.

SLOANE. I help out. On Saturdays.

ED. I see. I've been mistaken. (*Silence.*) Well, as I just said . . . I don't think it'd suit you. What with one thing and another. (*Pause.*) To show there's no hard feelings I'll make it worth your while. Call it a gift.

SLOANE. That's decent of you.

ED. Not at all. (*Pause.*) I'd like to give you a little present. Anything you care to name. Within reason.

SLOANE. What's within reason?

ED (*laughs*). Well . . . no . . . Jags. (*Laughs.*) . . . no sports cars. I'm not going as far as that.

SLOANE (*relaxing*). I was going to suggest an Aston Martin.

ED (*walks from the window looking for an ashtray. He does not find one*). I wish I could give you one, boy. I wish I could. (*Stubs out his cigarrette into a glass seashell on the sideboard.*) Are you a sports fan? Eh? Fond of sport? You look as though you might be. Look the . . . outdoor type, I'd say.

SLOANE. I am.

ED. I'd say you were. That's what struck me when you walked in. That's what puzzled me. She gave me the impression you were ... well, don't be offended ... I had the notion you were a shop assistant.

SLOANE. Never worked in a shop in my life.

ED. No. (*Pause.*) I see you're not that type. You're more of a ... as you might say ... the fresh air type.

SLOANE. I help out on Saturdays for a mate of mine. Len. You might know him. Lifeguard at the baths one time. Nice chap.

ED. You're fond of swimming?

SLOANE. I like a plunge now and then.

ED. Bodybuilding?

SLOANE. We had a nice little gym at the orphanage. Put me in all the teams they did. Relays ...

> ED *looks interested.*

... soccer ...

> ED *nods.*

... pole vault, ... long distance ...

> ED *opens his mouth.*

... 100 yards, discus, putting the shot.

> ED *rubs his hands together.*

Yes. yes. I'm an all rounder. A great all rounder. In anything you care to mention. Even in life.

> ED *lifts up a warning finger.*

... yes I like a good work out now and then.

ED. I used to do a lot of that at one time. With my mate ... we used to do all what you've just said. (*Pause.*) We were young. Innocent too. (*Shrugs. Pats his pocket. Takes out a packet of cigarettes. Smokes.*) All over now. (*Pause.*) Developing your muscles, eh? And character. (*Pause.*) . . . Well, well, well. (*Breathless.*) A little bodybuilder are you? I bet you are . . . (*Slowly.*) . . . do you . . . (*Shy.*) exercise regular?

SLOANE. As clockwork.

ED. Good, good. Stripped?

SLOANE. Fully.

ED. Complete. (*Striding to the window.*) How invigorating.

SLOANE. And I box. I'm a bit of a boxer.

ED. Ever done any wrestling?

SLOANE. On occasions.

ED. So, so.

SLOANE. I've got a full chest. Narrow hips. My biceps are –

ED. Do you wear leather . . . next to the skin? Leather jeans, say? Without . . . aah . . .

SLOANE. Pants?

ED (*laughs*). Get away! (*Pause.*) The question is are you clean living? You may as well know I set great store by morals. Too much of this casual bunking up nowadays. Too many lads being ruined by birds. I don't want you messing about with my sister.

SLOANE. I wouldn't.

ED. Have you made overtures to her?

SLOANE. No.

ED. Would you?

SLOANE. No.

ED. Not if circumstances were ripe?

SLOANE. Never.

ED. Does she disgust you?

SLOANE. Should she?

ED. It would be better if she did.

SLOANE. I've no interest in her.

Pause.

ED. I've a certain amount of influence. Friends with money. I've two cars. Judge for yourself. I generally spend my holidays in

places where the bints have got rings through their noses.
(*Pause*.) Women are like banks, boy, breaking and entering is a
serious business. Give me your word you're not vaginalatrous?

SLOANE. I'm not.

ED (*pause*). I'll believe you. Can you drive?

SLOANE. Yes.

ED. I might let you be my chauffeur.

SLOANE. Would you?

ED (*laughs*). We'll see . . . I could get you a uniform. Boots, pants,
a guaranteed 100 per cent no imitation jacket . . . an . . . er . . . a
white brushed nylon T-Shirt . . . with a little leather cap.
(*Laughs*.) Like that?

SLOANE *nods. Silence.*

Kip here a bit. Till we get settled. Come and see me. We'll
discuss salary arrangements and any other business. Here's my
card. (*Gives* SLOANE *a card*.) Have you seen my old dad?

SLOANE. I spoke to him.

ED. Wonderful for his age. (*Pause*.) Call her in will you?

SLOANE *exits.*

SLOANE (*off*). I think you're wanted. (*Re-enters*.)

ED. You'll find me a nice employer. (*Pause*.) When you come to
see me we must have a drink. A talk.

SLOANE. What about?

ED. Life. Sport. Love. Anything you care to name. Don't forget.

SLOANE. I'm looking forward to it.

ED. Do you drink?

SLOANE. When I'm not in training.

ED. You aren't in training at the moment, are you?

SLOANE. No.

ED. I wouldn't want you to break your training. Drinking I don't
mind. Drugs I abhor. You'll get to know all my habits.

KATH *enters,*

KATH. What you want?

ED. A word with you afore I go.

KATH. Are you staying, Mr Sloane?

ED. 'Course he's staying.

KATH. All right is it?

ED. He's going to work for me.

KATH (*pause*). He isn't going away is he?

ED. Offered him a job I have. I want a word with my sister, Sloane. Would you excuse us?

SLOANE *nods, smiles, and turns to go.*

KATH (*as he exits*). Have a meal, Mr Sloane. You'll find a quarter of boiled ham. Help yourself. You better have what's left 'cause I see he's been wolfing it. An' you heard me ask him to wait, di'n't you? I told him.

Exit SLOANE. *Silence.*

ED. You picked a nice lad there. Very nice. Clean. No doubt upright. A sports enthusiast. All the proper requisites. Don't take any money from him. I'll pay.

KATH. Can I buy him a shirt?

ED. What do you want to do that for?

KATH. His own mamma can't.

ED. He can buy his own clothes. Making yourself look ridiculous.

Pause.

KATH. When it's Christmas can I buy him a little gift?

ED. No.

KATH. Send him a card?

ED. Why?

KATH. I'd like to. I'd show you beforehand. (*Pause.*) Can I go to his mamma's grave?

ED. If you want. (*Pause.*) He'll laugh at you.

KATH. He wouldn't, Eddie.

Silence.

ED. I must go. I'll have a light meal. Take a couple of nembutal and then bed. I shall be out of town tomorrow.

KATH. Where?

ED. In Aylesbury. I shall dress in a quiet suit. Drive up in the motor. The Commissionaire will spring forward. There in that miracle of glass and concrete my colleagues and me will have a quiet drink before the business of the day.

KATH. Are your friends nice?

ED. Mature men.

KATH. No ladies?

Pause.

ED. What are you talking about? I live in a world of top decisions. We've no time for ladies.

KATH. Ladies are nice at a gathering.

ED. We don't want a lot of half-witted tarts.

KATH. They add colour and gaiety.

ED. Frightening everyone with their clothes.

Pause.

KATH. I hope you have a nice time. Perhaps one day you'll invite me to your hotel.

ED. I might.

KATH. Show me round.

ED. Yes.

KATH. Is it exquisitely furnished? High up?

ED. Very high. I see the river often.

A door slams.

Persuade the old man to speak to me.

KEMP (*off*). Is he gone?

KATH. Speak to him Dadda. He's something to ask you.

Silence.

ED (*petulant*). Isn't it incredible? I'm his only son. He won't see me. (*Goes to the door. Speaks through.*) I want a word with you.

(*Pause.*) Is he without human feelings? (*Pause. Brokenly.*) He won't speak to me. Has he no heart?

KATH. Come again.

ED. I'll get my lawyer to send a letter. If it's done legal he'll prove amenable. Give us a kiss. (*Kisses her. Pats her bottom.*) Be a good girl now. (*Exit.*)

KATH. Cheerio. (*Pause.*) I said Cheerio.

Door slams.

KATH (*goes to door*). Why don't you speak to him?

KEMP *enters. He does not reply.*

He invited me to his suite. The luxury takes your breath away. Money is no object. A waitress comes with the tea. (*Pause.*) I'm going to see him there one day. Speak to him Dadda.

KEMP. No.

KATH. Please.

KEMP. Never.

KATH. Let me phone saying you changed your mind.

KEMP. No

KATH. Let me phone.

KEMP. No.

KATH (*tearfully*). Oh, Dadda, you are unfair. If you don't speak to him he won't invite me to his suite. It's a condition. I won't be able to go. You found that address?

KEMP. I got lost, though.

KATH. Why didn't you ask? (*Pause.*) You had a tongue in your head. Oh, Dadda, you make me so angry with your silly ways. (*Pause.*) What was the house like?

KEMP. I didn't notice.

KATH. He said it was a hovel. A boy like him shouldn't be expected to live with the rougher elements. Do you know, Dadda, he has skin the like of which I never felt before. And he confesses to being an orphan. His story is so sad. I wept when I heard it. You know how soft-hearted I am.

Silence.

KEMP. I haven't been feeling well lately.

KATH. Have you seen the optician?

KEMP. My eyes are getting much worse.

KATH. Without a word of a lie you are like a little child.

KEMP. I'm all alone.

KATH. You have me.

KEMP. He may take you away.

KATH. Where to?

KEMP. Edinburgh.

KATH. Too cold.

KEMP. Or Bournemouth. You always said you'd go somewhere with palms.

KATH. I'd always consult you first.

KEMP. You'd put me in a home. (*Pause.*) Would you be tempted?

Silence.

KATH. You ought to consult an oculist. See your oculist at once. (*Pause.*) Go to bed. I'll bring you a drinkie. In the morning you'll feel different.

KEMP. You don't love me.

KATH. I've never stopped loving you.

KEMP. I'm going to die, Kath . . . I'm dying.

KATH (*angrily*). You've been at that ham haven't you? Half a jar of pickles you've put away. Don't moan to me if you're up half the night with the tummy ache. I've got no sympathy for you.

KEMP. Goodnight then.

KATH (*watches him out of the door. Looks through into the kitchen*). All right, Mr Sloane? Help yourself . . . all right? (*Comes back into the room. Takes lamp from sideboard and puts it on to table beside settee. Goes to record player, puts on record. Pulls curtains across alcove and disappears behind them. The stage is empty. The record plays for a few seconds and then the needle jumps a groove, slides across record. Automatic change switches record off.* KATH *pokes her head from behind curtain, looks at record player, disappears again. Re-appears wearing a transparent négligé. Picks up aerosol spray, sprays room. Calls through door*). Have you finished, Mr Sloane, dear?

SLOANE (*off*). Ugh?

KATH. You have? I'm so glad. I don't want to disturb you at your food. (*Sees knitting on sideboard, picks it up.*) Come into the lounge if you wish. I'm just at a quiet bit of knitting before I go to bed.

SLOANE *enters wiping his mouth.*

A lovely piece of ham, wasn't it?

SLOANE. Lovely.

KATH. I'll give you a splendid breakfast in the morning. (*Realizes that there is only one needle in the knitting. Searches in the junk and finds the other. Takes it to the settee.* SLOANE *sits on one end.*) (*Pause.*) Isn't this room gorgeous?

SLOANE. Yes.

KATH. That vase over there come from Bombay. Do you have any interest in that part of the world?

SLOANE. I like Dieppe.

KATH. Ah . . . it's all the same. I don't suppose they know the difference themselves. Are you comfortable? Let me plump your cushion. (*Plumps a cushion behind his head. Laughs lightly.*) I really by rights should ask you to change places. This light is showing me up. (*Pause.*) I blame it on the manufacturers. They make garments so thin nowadays you'd think they intended to provoke a rape.

Pause.

Sure you're comfy? (*Leans over him.*)

SLOANE *pulls her hand towards him. She laughs, half in panic.*

SLOANE. You're a teaser ent you?

KATH (*breaks away*). I hope I'm not. I was trying to find the letter from my little boy's father. I treasure it. But I seem to have mislaid it. I found a lot of photos though.

SLOANE. Yes.

KATH. Are you interested in looking through them? (*Brings the snapshots over.*)

SLOANE. Are they him?

KATH. My lover.

SLOANE. Bit blurred.

KATH. It brings back memories. He reminds me of you. (*Pause.*) He too was handsome and in the prime of manhood. Can you wonder I fell. (*Pause.*) I wish he were here now to love and protect me. (*Leans her arm on his shoulder. Shows him another snap.*) This is me. I was younger then.

SLOANE. Smart.

KATH. Yes my hair was nice.

SLOANE. Yes.

KATH. An' this . . . I don't know whether I ought to let you see it.

SLOANE *attempts to seize it.*

Now then!

He takes it from her.

SLOANE. A seat in a wood?

KATH. That seat is erected to the memory of Mrs Gwen Lewis. She was a lady who took a lot of trouble with invalids. (*Pause.*) It was near that seat that my baby was thought of.

SLOANE. On that seat?

KATH (*shyly*). Not on it exactly. Nearby . . .

SLOANE. In the bushes? . . .

She giggles.

KATH. Yes. (*Pause.*) He was rough with me.

SLOANE. Uncomfortable, eh?

KATH. I couldn't describe my feelings. (*Pause.*) I don't think the fastening on this thing I'm wearing will last much longer. (*The snapshots slip from her hand.*) There! you've knocked the photos on the floor.

(*Pause: he attempts to move; she is almost on top of him.*) Mr Sloane . . . (*Rolls on to him.*) You should wear more clothes, Mr Sloane. I believe you're as naked as me. And there's no excuse for it. (*Silence.*) I'll be your mamma. I need to be loved. Gently. Oh! I shall be so ashamed in the morning. (*Switches off the light.*) What a big heavy baby you are. Such a big heavy baby.

CURTAIN

ACT TWO

Some months later. Morning.

SLOANE *is lying on the settee wearing boots, leather trousers and a white T-shirt. A newspaper covers his face.* KATH *enters. Looks at the settee.*

SLOANE. Where you been?

KATH. Shopping, dear. Did you want me?

SLOANE. I couldn't find you.

KATH (*goes to the window. Takes off her headscarf*). What's Eddie doing?

SLOANE. A bit of serviceing.

KATH. But that's your job.

SLOANE *removes the newspaper.*

He shouldn't do your work.

SLOANE. I was on the beer. My guts is playing up.

KATH. Poor boy. (*Pause.*) Go and help him. For mamma's sake.

SLOANE. I may go in a bit.

KATH. He's a good employer. Studies your interests. You want to think of his position. He's proud of it. Now you're working for him his position is your position. (*Pause.*) Go and give him a hand.

SLOANE. No.

KATH. Are you too tired?

SLOANE. Yes.

KATH. We must make allowances for you. You're young. (*Pause.*) You're not taking advantage are you?

SLOANE. No.

KATH: I know you aren't. When you've had a drinkie go and help him.

SLOANE. If you want.

Pause.

KATH. Did mamma hear you were on the razzle?

SLOANE. Yes.

KATH. Did you go up West? You were late coming home. (*Pause.*) Very late.

SLOANE. Three of my mates and me had a night out.

KATH. Are they nice boys?

SLOANE. We have interests in common.

KATH. They aren't roughs are they? Mamma doesn't like you associating with them.

SLOANE. Not on your life. They're gentle. Refined youths. Thorpe, Beck and Doolan. We toured the nighteries in the motor.

KATH. Was Ed with you?

SLOANE. No.

KATH. Did you ask him? He would have come.

SLOANE. He was tired. A hard day yesterday.

KATH. Ask him next time.

Pause.

SLOANE. We ended up at a fabulous place. Soft music, pink shades, lovely atmosphere.

KATH. I hope you behaved yourself.

SLOANE. One of the hostesses gave me her number. Told me to ring her.

KATH. Take no notice of her. She might not be nice.

SLOANE. Not nice?

KATH. She might be a party girl.

Pause.

SLOANE. What exactly do you mean?

KATH. Mamma worries for you.

SLOANE. You're attempting to run my life.

KATH. Is baby cross?

SLOANE. You're developing distinctly possessive tendencies.

KATH. You can get into trouble saying that.

SLOANE. A possessive woman.

KATH. A mamma can't be possessive.

SLOANE. Can't she?

KATH. You know she can't. You're being naughty.

SLOANE. Never heard of a possessive mum?

KATH. Stop it. It's rude. Did she teach you to say that?

SLOANE. What?

KATH. What you just said.

> SLOANE *makes no reply*.

You're spoiling yourself in my eyes, Mr Sloane. You won't ring this girl will you?

SLOANE. I haven't decided.

KATH. Decide now. To please me. I don't know what you see in these girls. You have your friends for company.

SLOANE. They're boys.

KATH. What's wrong with them? You can talk freely. Not like with a lady.

SLOANE. I don't want to talk.

> *Pause.*

KATH. She might be after your money.

SLOANE. I haven't got any.

KATH. But Eddie has. She might be after his.

SLOANE. Look, you're speaking of a very good class bird.

KATH. I have to protect you, baby, because you're easily led.

SLOANE. I like being led. (*Pause.*) I need to be let out occasionally. Off the lead.

> *Pause.*

KATH. She'll make you ill.

SLOANE. Shut it. (*Pause.*) Make me ill!

KATH. Girls do.

SLOANE. How dare you. Making filthy insinuations. I won't have it. You disgust me you do. Standing there without your teeth. Why don't you get smartened up? Get a new rig-out.

Pause.

KATH. Do I disgust you?

SLOANE. Yes.

KATH. Honest?

SLOANE. And truly. You horrify me. (*Pause.*) You think I'm kidding. I'll give up my room if you don't watch out.

KATH. Oh, no!

SLOANE. Clear out.

KATH. Don't think of such drastic action. I'd never forgive myself if I drove you away. (*Pause.*) I won't any more.

He attempts to rise.

KATH (*takes his hand*). Don't go, dear. Stay with me while I collect myself. I've been upset and I need comfort. (*Silence.*) Are you still disgusted?

SLOANE. A bit.

KATH (*takes his hand, presses it to her lips*). Sorry baby. Better?

SLOANE. Mmmm.

Silence.

KATH. How good you are to me.

KEMP *enters. He carries a stick. Taps his way to the sideboard.*

My teeth, since you mentioned the subject, Mr Sloane, are in the kitchen in Steigene. Usually I allow a good soak overnight. But what with one thing and another I forgot. Otherwise I would never be in such a state. (*Pause.*) I hate people who are careless with their dentures.

KEMP *opens a drawer.*

KEMP. Seen my tablets?

KATH. If you're bad go to bed.

KEMP. I need one o' my pills.

He picks his way through the junk.

SLOANE (*goes over to him*). What you want?

KEMP. Let me alone.

SLOANE. Tell me what you want.

KEMP. I don't want no help. (*Pause.*) I'm managing.

SLOANE. Let me know what you want and I'll look for it.

KEMP. I can manage.

SLOANE *goes back to the settee. Silence.*

KATH. What a lot of foreigners there are about lately. I see one today. Playing the accordion. They live in a world of their own these people.

KEMP. Coloured?

KATH. No.

KEMP. I expect he was. They do come over here. Raping people. It's a problem. Just come out o' jail had he?

KATH. I really didn't stop long enough to ask. I just commented on the tune he was playing.

KEMP. Oh, they're all for that.

KATH (*leans over SLOANE*). Mamma has something special to say to you.

KEMP. All for that.

SLOANE (*touches her hair*). What?

KATH (*to KEMP, louder*). I don't think he was dark enough to be coloured, Dadda. Honestly I don't.

KEMP. They should send them back.

SLOANE. What's your news?

KATH. Can't you guess.

SLOANE. No.

KATH. I know you can't.

KEMP. You should've put in a complaint.

KATH. Oh, no Dadda.

KEMP. Playing his bloody music in the street.

KATH. What language! You should be a splendid example to us. Instead of which you carry on like a common workman. Don't swear like that in my presence again.

Silence. SLOANE *attempts to grab her shopping bag. She rises,* SLOANE *touches her up. She grunts. Smacks his hand.*

KEMP. What's up?

KATH. Nothing. Aren't the tulips glorious this year by the municipal offices. What a brave showing. They must spend a fortune.

SLOANE. What have you bought me?

KATH. Mamma is going to have a . . . (*Makes a rocking motion with her arms.*)

SLOANE. What? (*Pause.*) What?

KATH. A little – (*Looks over to* KEMP. *Makes the motion of rocking a baby in her arms. Purses her lips. Blows a kiss.*)

SLOANE *sits up. Points to himself.*

KATH (*nods her head. Presses her mouth to his ear : whispers*). A baby brother.

KEMP. What are you having?

KATH. A . . . bath, Dadda. You know that woman from the shops? (*Pause.*) You wouldn't believe what a ridiculous spectacle she's making of herself.

KEMP. Oh.

KATH (*to* SLOANE). 'Course it's ever so dangerous at my age. But doctor thinks it'll be all right.

SLOANE. Sure.

KATH. I was worried in case you'd be cross.

SLOANE. We mustn't let anyone know.

KATH. It's our secret. (*Pause.*) I'm excited.

KEMP. Are you having it after tea, Kath?

KATH. Why?

KEMP. I thought of having one as well. Are you there?

KATH. Yes.

KEMP. Have you seen them pills?

KATH. Have I seen his pills. They're where you left them I expect.
(*Goes to the sideboard. Finds bottle. Gives it to* KEMP.) How
many you had today?

KEMP. Two.

KATH. They're not meant to be eaten like sweets you know.

He exits.

I been to the Register Office.

SLOANE. What for?

KATH. To inquire about the licence.

SLOANE. Who?

KATH. You

SLOANE. Who to?

KATH. Me. Don't you want to? You wouldn't abandon me? Leave
me to face the music.

SLOANE. What music?

KATH. When Eddie hears.

SLOANE. He mustn't hear.

KATH. Baby, how can we stop him?

SLOANE. He'd kill me. I'd be out of a job.

KATH. I suppose we couldn't rely on him employing you any
longer.

SLOANE. Don't say anything. I'll see a man I know.

KATH. What? But I'm looking forward to having a new little
brother.

SLOANE. Out of the question.

KATH. Please . . .

SLOANE. No. In any case I couldn't marry you. I'm not the type.
And all things being equal I may not be living here much
longer.

KATH. Aren't you comfy in your bed?

SLOANE. Yes.

KATH (*folds her arms round him. Kisses his head*). We could marry in secret. Couldn't you give me something, baby? So's I feel in my mind we were married?

SLOANE. What like?

KATH. A ring. Or a bracelet? You got a nice locket. I noticed it. Make me a present of that.

SLOANE. I can't do that.

KATH. As a token of your esteem. So's I feel I belong to you.

SLOANE. It belonged to my mum.

KATH. I'm your mamma now.

SLOANE. No.

KATH. Go on.

SLOANE. But it was left to me.

KATH. You mustn't cling to old memories. I shall begin to think you don't love mamma.

SLOANE. I do.

KATH. Then give me that present. (*Unhooks the chain.*) Ta.

SLOANE. I hate parting with it.

KATH. I'll wear it for ever.

> ED *enters. Stands smoking a cigarette. Turns. Exits. Re-enters with a cardboard box.*

ED. This yours?

KATH (*goes over. Looks in the box*). It's my gnome.

ED. They just delivered it.

KATH. The bad weather damaged him. His little hat come off. I sent him to the Gnomes' Hospital to be repaired.

ED. Damaged, was he?

KATH. Yes.

ED. Well, well. (*Pause.*) It's monkey weather out there.

SLOANE. I wasn't cold.

ED. You're young. Healthy. Don't feel the cold, do you?

SLOANE. No.

ED. Not at all?

SLOANE. Sometimes.

ED. Not often. (*Pause.*) I expect it's all that orange juice.

KATH. Mr Sloane was coming out, Eddie. I assure you.

ED. I know that. I can trust him.

KATH. You've a lovely colour. Let me feel your hand. Why it's freezing. You feel his hand, Mr Sloane.

ED. He doesn't want to feel my hand. (*Pause.*) When you're ready, boy, we'll go.

SLOANE. Check the oil?

ED. Mmn.

SLOANE. Petrol?

ED. Mmn. (*Pause.*) Down, en it?

SLOANE. Down?

ED. From yesterday. We filled her up yesterday.

SLOANE. Did we? Was it yesterday?

ED. Mmn. (*Pause.*) We used a lot since then.

SLOANE. You ought to get yourself a new car. It eats petrol.

Pause.

ED. Maybe you're right. You didn't use it last night, did you?

SLOANE. Me?

ED. I thought you might have.

SLOANE. No.

ED. Funny.

Silence.

KATH. I see a woolly in Boyce's, Mr Sloane. I'm giving it you as a birthday present.

ED. What do you want to do that for?

KATH. Mr Sloane won't mind.

ED. Chucking money about.

KATH. Mr Sloane doesn't mind me. He's one of the family.

ED. Hark at it. Shove up, boy.

SLOANE (*moves*). Sit by me.

ED (*sits next to him*). You didn't use my motor last night then?

SLOANE. No.

ED. That's all I wanted. As long as you're telling the truth, boy.

He takes SLOANE'*s hand.*

You've an honest hand. Square. What a grip you got.

SLOANE. I'm improving.

ED. Yes, I can tell that. You've grown bolder since we met. Bigger and bolder. Don't get too bold will you? Eh? (*Laughs.*) I'm going to buy you something for your birthday as well.

SLOANE. Can I rely on it?

ED. Aah.

SLOANE. Will it be expensive?

ED. Very. I might consider lashing out a bit and buying you a . . . um, er, aahhh . . .

SLOANE. Thank you. Thank you.

ED. Don't thank me. Thank yourself. You deserve it.

SLOANE. I think I do.

ED. I think you do. Go and put that box in the kitchen.

KATH. It's no trouble, Eddie.

ED. Let the boy show you politeness.

KATH. But he does. Often. He's often polite to me.

SLOANE *picks up the box and exits.*

KATH. I never complain.

Pause.

ED. Where was he last night?

KATH. He watched the telly. A programme where people guessed each other's names.

ED. What else?

KATH. Nothing else.

ED. He used the car last night.

KATH. No.

Pause.

ED. If he's not careful he can have his cards.

KATH. He's only young.

ED. Joy-riding in my motor.

KATH. He's a good boy.

ED. Act your age. (*Pause.*) Encouraging him. I've watched you. What you want to keep him in here for all morning?

KATH. I didn't want him here. I told him to go and help you.

ED. You did? And he wouldn't?

KATH. No. Yes.

ED. What do you mean?

KATH. I thought it was his rest period, Eddie. You do give him a rest sometimes. I know, 'cause you're a good employer. (*Sits beside him.*)

ED. What do I pay him for?

KATH. To keep him occupied, I suppose.

ED (*makes no reply. At last, irritated*). You're a pest, you are.

KATH. I'm sorry.

ED (*glances at her*). Keeping him in when he ought to be at work. How do you expect him to work well with you messing about?

KATH. He was just coming.

ED. Taking him from his duty. Wasting my money.

KATH. I won't any more.

ED. It's too late. I'll pay him off. Not satisfactory.

KATH. No.

ED. Not the type of person that I had expected.

KATH. He likes his work.

ED. He can go elsewhere.

KATH. He's a great help to me. I shall cry if he goes away. (*Pause.*) I shall have to take a sedative.

ED. I'll find someone else for you.

KATH. No.

ED. An older man. With more maturity.

KATH. I want my baby.

ED. Your what?

KATH. I'm his mamma and he appreciates me. (*Pause.*) He told me.

ED. When? When?

KATH. I can't remember.

ED. He loves you?

KATH. No, I didn't say that. But he calls me mamma. I love him 'cause I have no little boy of my own. And if you send him away I shall cry like the time you took my real baby.

ED. You were wicked then.

KATH. I know.

ED. Being rude. Ruining my little matie. Teaching him nasty things. That's why I sent it away. (*Pause.*) You're not doing rude things with this kiddy, are you, like you did with Tommy?

KATH. No.

ED. Sure?

KATH. I love him like a mamma.

ED. I can't trust you.

KATH. I'm a trustworthy lady.

ED. Allowing him to kip here was a mistake.

Silence.

KATH. I never wanted to do rude things. Tommy made me.

ED. Liar!

KATH. Insisted. Pestered me he did. All summer.

ED. You're a liar.

KATH. Am I?

ED. He didn't want anything to do with you. He told me that.

KATH. You're making it up.

ED. I'm not.

KATH. He loved me.

ED. He didn't.

KATH. He wanted to marry me.

ED. Marry you? You're a ridiculous figure and no mistake.

KATH. He'd have married me only his folks were against it.

ED. I always imagined you were an intelligent woman. I find you're not.

KATH. He said they was.

ED. Did he? When?

KATH. When the stork was coming.

ED (*laughs*). Well, well. Fancy you remembering. You must have a long memory.

KATH. I have.

ED. Let me disillusion you.

KATH. Don't hurt me, Eddie.

ED. You need hurting, you do. Mr and Mrs Albion Bolter were quite ready to have you marry Tommy.

KATH. No they wasn't.

ED. Allow me to know.

KATH (*pause*). He wouldn't have lied, Ed. You're telling stories.

ED. I'm not.

KATH. But he said it was 'cause I was poor. (*Pause.*) I couldn't fit into the social background demanded of him. His duty came between us.

ED. You could have been educated. Gone to beauty salons. Learned to speak well.

KATH. No.

ED. They wanted you to marry him. Tommy and me had our first set-to about it. You should have heard the language he used to me.

KATH. I was loved. How can you say that?

ED. Forget it.

KATH. He sent me the letter I treasure.

ED. I burned it.

Pause.

KATH. It was his last words to me.

ED. And that kiddy out there. I'm not having him go the same way.

KATH *goes to the window.*

KATH. Did you burn my letter?

ED. Yes. (*Pause.*) And that old photo as well. I thought you was taking an unhealthy interest in the past.

KATH. The photo as well?

ED. You forget it.

KATH. I promised to show it to someone. I wondered why I couldn't find it.

ED. You wicked girl.

KATH. I'm not wicked. I think you're wicked. (*Sniffs without dignity.*)

ED (*lights a cigarette. Looks at her*). While I'm at it I'll get the old man to look at those papers. (*Pause.*) Get my case in, will you?

She does not reply. He stands up. Exits. Returns with briefcase.

I made a mark where he's to sign. On the dotted line. (*Laughs.*) I'll be glad when it's over. To use an expression foreign to my nature – I'll be bloody glad. (*Stares at* KATH *as she continues to cry. Turns away. Pause.*) Quit bawling, will you?

KATH *blows her nose on the edge of her apron.*

You should be like me. You'd have something to cry over then, if you got responsibilities like me. (*Silence.*) Haven't you got a hankie? You don't want the boy to see you like that? (*Silence.*)

SLOANE *enters.*

Put it away, did you?

SLOANE. Yes.

ED. That's a good boy.

Pause.

KATH. Mr Sloane.

SLOANE. What?

KATH. Can *I* call you Boy?

SLOANE. I don't think you'd better.

KATH. Why not?

ED. I'm his employer, see. He knows that you're only his landlady.

SLOANE *smiles.*

KATH. I don't mean in front of strangers. (*Pause.*) I'd be sparing with the use of the name.

ED. No! (*Sharply.*) Haven't you got anything to do? Standing there all day.

KATH *exits.*

Getting fat as a pig, she is.

SLOANE. Is she?

ED. Not noticed?

SLOANE. No.

ED. I have.

SLOANE. How old is she?

ED. Forty-one. (*Shrugs.*) Forty-two. She ought to slim. I'd advise that.

SLOANE. She's . . .

ED. She's like a sow. Though she is my sister.

SLOANE. She's not bad.

ED. No?

SLOANE. I don't think so.

ED *goes to the window. Stands. Lost. Pause.*

ED. Where was you last night?

SLOANE. I told you –

ED. I know what you told me. A pack of lies. D'you think I'm an idiot or something?

SLOANE. No.

ED. I want the truth.

SLOANE. I went for a spin. I had a headache.

ED. Where did you go?

SLOANE. Along the A40.

ED. Who went with you?

SLOANE. Nobody.

ED. Are you being entirely honest?

Pause.

SLOANE. Three mates come with me.

ED. They had headaches too?

SLOANE. I never asked.

ED. Cheeky. (*Pause.*) Who are they? Would I want them in my motor?

SLOANE. You'd recognize Harry Thorpe. Small, clear complexioned, infectious good humour.

ED. I might.

SLOANE. Harry Beck I brought up one night. A Wednesday it was. But Dooloan no. You wouldn't know him.

ED. Riding round in my motor all night, eh?

SLOANE. I'd challenge that.

ED. What type of youth are they?

SLOANE. Impeccable taste. Buy their clothes up West.

ED. Any of them wear lipstick?

SLOANE. Certainly not.

ED. You'd notice, would you? (*Throws over a lipstick.*) What's this doing in the back of the motor?

> *Silence.*

SLOANE (*laughs*). Oh . . . you jogged my memory . . . yes . . . Doolan's married . . . an' we took his wife along.

ED. Can't you do better than that?

SLOANE. Straight up.

ED (*emotionally*). Oh, boy . . . Taking birds out in my motor.

SLOANE. Would you accept an unconditional apology.

ED. Telling me lies.

SLOANE. It won't happen again.

ED. What are your feelings towards me?

SLOANE. I respect you.

ED. Is that the truth?

SLOANE. Honest.

ED. Then why tell me lies?

SLOANE. That's only your impression.

> *Pause.*

ED. Was this an isolated incident?

SLOANE. This is the first time.

ED. Really.

SLOANE. Yes. Can you believe me?

Pause.

ED. I believe you. I believe you're regretting the incident already. But don't repeat it. (*Silence.*) Or next time I won't be so lenient. (*Pause.*) I think the time has come for us to make a change.

SLOANE. In what way?

ED. I need you on tap.

SLOANE. Mmmn . . .

Pause.

ED. At all hours. In case I have to make a journey to a distant place at an unexpected and inconvenient hour of the night. In a manner of speaking it's urgent.

SLOANE. Of course.

ED. I got work to do. (*Pause.*) I think it would be best if you leave here today.

SLOANE. It might be.

ED. Give it a trial. (*Pause.*) You see my way of looking at it?

SLOANE. Sure.

ED. And you shouldn't be left with her. She's no good. No good at all. A crafty tart she is. I could tell you things about – the way these women carry on. (*Pause.*) Especially her. (*Opens window. Throws cigarette out.*) These women do you no good. I can tell you that. (*Feels in his coat pocket. Takes out a packet of mints. Puts one in his mouth. Pause.*) One of sixteen come up to me the other day – which is a thing I never expected, come up to me and said she'd been given my address. I don't know whether it was a joke or something. You see that sort of thing . . .

SLOANE. Well . . .?

ED. You could check it.

SLOANE. I'd be pleased.

ED. Certainly. I got feelings.

SLOANE. You're sensitive. You can't be bothered.

ED. You got it wrong when you says that. I seen birds all shapes and sizes and I'm most certainly not . . . um . . . ah . . . sensitive.

SLOANE. No?

ED. I just don't give a monkey's fart.

SLOANE. It's a legitimate position.

ED. But I can deal with them same as you.

SLOANE. I'm glad to hear it.

ED. What's your opinion of the way these women carry on?

Pause.

SLOANE. I feel . . . how would you say?

ED. Don't you think they're crude?

SLOANE. Occasionally. In a way.

ED. You never know where you are with half of them.

SLOANE. All the same it's necessary.

ED. Ah well, you're talking of a different subject entirely. It's necessary. Occasionally. But it's got to be kept within bounds.

SLOANE. I'm with you there. All the way.

ED (*laughs*). I've seen funny things happen and no mistake. The way these birds treat decent fellows. I hope you never get serious with one. What a life. Backache, headache or her mum told her never to when there's an 'R' in the month. (*Pause. Stares from window.*) How do you feel then?

SLOANE. On the main points we agree.

ED. Pack your bags.

SLOANE. Now?

ED. Immediate.

SLOANE. Will I get a rise in pay?

ED. A rise?

SLOANE. My new situation calls for it.

ED. You already had two.

SLOANE. They were tokens. I'd like you to upgrade my salary. How about a little car?

ED. That's a bit (*laughs*) of an unusual request en it?

SLOANE. You could manage it.

ED. It all costs money. I tell you what – I'll promise you one for Christmas.

SLOANE. This year?

ED. Or next year.

SLOANE. It's a date.

ED. You and me. That's the life, boy. Without doubt I'm glad I met you.

SLOANE. Are you?

ED. I see you had possibilities from the start. You had an air. (*Pause.*) A way with you.

SLOANE. Something about me.

ED. That's it. The perfect phrase. Personality.

SLOANE. Really?

ED. That's why I don't want you living here. Wicked waste. I'm going to tell you something. Prepare to raise your eyebrows.

SLOANE. Yes.

ED. She had a kiddy once.

SLOANE. Go on.

ED. That's right. On the wrong side of the blanket.

SLOANE. Your sister?

ED. I had a matie. What times we had. Fished. Swam. Rolled home pissed at two in the morning. We were innocent I tell you. Until she came on the scene. (*Pause.*) Teaching him things he shouldn't 'a done. It was over . . . gone . . . finished. (*Clears his throat.*) She got him to put her in the family way that's what I always maintain. Nothing was the same after. Not ever. A typical story.

SLOANE. Sad, though.

ED. Yes it is. I should say. Of course in a way of looking at it it laid the foundation of my success. I put him to one side which was difficult because he was alluring. I managed it though. Got a grip on myself. And finally become a success. (*Pause.*) That's no mean achievement, is it?

SLOANE. No.

ED. I'm proud.

SLOANE. Why shouldn't you be?

ED. I'm the possessor of two bank accounts. Respected in my own right. And all because I turned my back on him. Does that impress you?

SLOANE. It impresses me.

ED. I have no hesitation in saying that it was worth it. None.

The door opens slowly, KEMP *stands waiting, staring in, listening.*

SLOANE. What is it, Pop?

KEMP *enters the room, listens, backs to the door. Stops.*

KEMP. Is Ed there with you? (*Pause.*) Ed?

ED (*with emotion*). Dad . . . (*He goes to* KEMP, *puts an arm round his shoulder.*) What's come over you?

KEMP *clutches* ED's *coat, almost falls to his knees.* ED *supports him.*

Don't kneel to me. I forgive you. I'm the one to kneel.

KEMP. No, no.

ED. Pat me on the head. Pronounce a blessing. Forgive and forget, eh? I'm sorry and so are you.

KEMP. I want a word with you. (*He squints in* SLOANE's *direction.*) Something to tell you.

ED. Words, Dad. A string of words. We're together again.

Pause.

KEMP. Tell him to go.

ED. Dad, what manners you got. How rude you've become.

KEMP. I got business to discuss.

SLOANE. He can speak in front of me, can't he, Ed?

ED. I've no secrets from the boy.

KEMP. It's personal.

SLOANE. I'd like to stay Ed . . . in case . . .

KEMP. I'm not talking in front of him.

SLOANE. Pop . . . (*laughs*) . . . Ed will tell me afterwards. See if he doesn't.

Pause.

KEMP. I want to talk in private.

ED *nods at the door,* SLOANE *shrugs.*

SLOANE. Give in to him, eh, Ed? (*Laughs.*) You know, Pop . . . well . . . (*Pause.*) O.K., have it your own way. (*Exits.*)

KEMP. Is he gone?

ED. What's the matter with you?

KEMP. That kid – who is he?

ED. He's lived here six months. Where have you been?

KEMP. What's his background?

ED. He's had a hard life, dad. Struggles. I have his word for it. An orphan deserves our sympathy.

KEMP. You like him?

ED. One of the best.

Silence.

KEMP. He comes to my room at night.

ED. He's being friendly.

KEMP. I can't get to sleep. He talks all the time.

ED. Give an example of his conversation. What does he talk about?

KEMP. Goes on and on. (*Pause.*) An' he makes things up about

me. (*He rolls up his sleeve, shows a bruise.*) Give me a thumping, he did.

ED. When? (*Pause.*) Can't you remember?

KEMP. Before the weekend.

ED. Did you complain?

KEMP. I can't sleep for worry. He comes in and stands by my bed in the dark. In his pyjamas.

Pause.

ED. I'll have a word with him.

KEMP (*lifts his trouser leg, pulls down his sock, shows an Elastoplast*). He kicked me yesterday.

SLOANE (*appears in the doorway*). There's a man outside wants a word with you, Pop. (*Pause.*) Urgent he says.

KEMP. Tell him to wait.

SLOANE. How long?

KEMP. Tell him to wait will you?

SLOANE. It's urgent.

KEMP. What's his name?

SLOANE. Grove. Or Greeves, I don't know.

KEMP. I don't know nobody called that.

SLOANE. He's on about the . . . (*Pause*) . . . whether he can dump something. You'd better see him.

KEMP (*swings round, tries to bring* SLOANE *into focus*). Oh . . .

ED (*nods, winks*). In a minute, boy.

SLOANE *closes door, exits.*

Silence.

ED. Dad . . .

KEMP. He's in bed with her most nights. People talk. The woman from the shop spotted it first. Four months gone, she reckons.

Pause.

ED. That's interesting.

KEMP. She's like the side of a house lately. It's not what she eats. (*Silence.*) Shall I tell you something else?

ED. Don't.

Pause.

KEMP. He's got it in for me.

ED. . . don't – tell me anything –

KEMP. It's because I'm a witness. To his crime.

ED. What crime.

SLOANE (*enters carrying a suitcase. Puts it on the table. Opens it*). Man en half creating, Pop. You ought to see to him. Jones or Greeves or whatever his name is. He's out the back.

ED. Go and see to him, Dad. (SLOANE *exits*.) See this man, Dad. Go on.

KEMP. There's no man there.

ED. How do you know? You haven't been and looked have you?

KEMP. It's a blind. (*Pause*.) Let me tell you about the boy.

ED. I don't want to hear. (*Pause*.) I'm surprised to find you spreading stories about the kiddy. Shocked. (SLOANE *returns with a pile of clothes*.) That's slander. You'll find yourself in queer street. (SLOANE *begins to pack the case*.) Apologize. (KEMP *shakes his head*.) The old man's got something to say to you, boy.

SLOANE (*smiling*). Oh, yes?

ED (*to* KEMP). Haven't you? (*Pause*.) Do you talk to him much? Is he talkative at night?

SLOANE. We have the odd confab sometimes. As I dawdle over my cocoa.

ED. You go and talk to that man, Dad. See if you can't get some sense into him. Dumping their old shit back of the house.

They watch KEMP *exit.*
Silence.

ED. He's just been putting in a complaint.

SLOANE. About me?

ED. I can't take it serious. He more or less said you . . . well, in so many words he said . . .

SLOANE. Really?

ED. Did you ever kick him?

SLOANE. Sometimes. He understands.

ED. An' he said . . . Is she pregnant?

Pause.

SLOANE. Who?

ED. Deny it, boy. Convince me it isn't true.

SLOANE. Why?

ED. So's I – (*Pause.*) Lie to me.

SLOANE. Why should I?

ED. It's true then? Have you been messing with her?

SLOANE. She threw herself at me.

Silence.

ED. What a little whoreson you are you little whoreson. You are a little whoreson and no mistake. I'm put out my boy. Choked. (*Pause.*) What attracted you? Did she give trading stamps? You're like all these layabouts. Kiddies with no fixed abode.

SLOANE. I put up a fight.

ED. She had your cherry?

SLOANE. No.

ED. Not the first time?

SLOANE. No.

ED. Or the second?

SLOANE. No.

ED. Dare I go on?

SLOANE. It's my upbringing. Lack of training. No proper parental control.

ED. I'm sorry for you.

SLOANE. I'm glad of that. I wouldn't want to upset you.

ED. That does you credit.

SLOANE. You've no idea what I've been through. (*Pause.*) I prayed for guidance.

ED. I'd imagine the prayer for your situation would be hard to come by. (*Pause.*) Did you never think of locking your bedroom door?

SLOANE. She'd think I'd gone mad.

ED. Why didn't you come to me?

SLOANE. It's not the kind of thing I could –

ED. I'd've been your confessor.

SLOANE. You don't understand. It gathered momentum.

ED. You make her sound like a washing machine. When did you stop?

SLOANE. I haven't stopped.

ED. Not stopped yet?

SLOANE. Here, lay off.

ED. What a ruffian.

SLOANE. I got my feelings.

ED. You were stronger than her. Why didn't you put up a struggle?

SLOANE. I was worn out. I was overwrought. Nervous. On edge.

Pause.

ED. You're a constant source of amazement, boy, a never ending tale of infamy. I'd hardly credit it. A kid of your age. Joy-riding in an expensive car, a woman pregnant. My word, you're unforgivable. (*Pause.*) I don't know whether I'm qualified to pronounce judgement.

Pause.

SLOANE. I'm easily led. I been dogged by bad luck.

ED. You've got to learn to live a decent life sometime, boy. I blame the way you are on emotional shock. So perhaps (*Pause*) we ought to give you another chance.

SLOANE. That's what I says.

ED. Are you confused?

SLOANE. I shouldn't be surprised.

ED. Never went to church? Correct me if I'm wrong.

SLOANE. You got it, Ed. Know me better than I know myself.

ED. Your youth pleads for leniency and, by God, I'm going to give it. You're pure as the Lamb. Purer.

SLOANE. Am I forgiven?

ED. Will you reform?

SLOANE. I swear it . . . Ed, look at me. Speak a few words of forgiveness. (*Pause.*) Pity me.

ED. I do.

SLOANE. Oh, Ed, you're a pal.

ED. Am I?

SLOANE. One of my mates.

ED. Is that a fact? How refreshing to hear you say it.

SLOANE. You've a generous nature.

ED. You could say that. I don't condemn out of hand like some.
   But do me a favour – avoid the birds in future. That's what's
   been your trouble.

SLOANE. It has.

ED. She's to blame.

SLOANE. I've no hesitation in saying that.

ED. Why conform to the standards of the cowshed? (*Pause.*) It's
   a thing you grow out of. With me behind you, boy, you'll grow
   out of it.

SLOANE. Thanks.

ED. Your hand on it. (SLOANE *holds out his hand.* ED *takes it, holds
   it for a long time, searches* SLOANE's *face.*) I think you're a good
   boy. (*Silence.*) I knew there must be some reasonable explanation
   for your otherwise inexplicable conduct. I'll have a word with
   the old man.

SLOANE. Gets on my nerves he does.

ED. Has he been tormenting you?

SLOANE. I seriously consider leaving as a result of the way he
   carries on.

ED. Insults?

SLOANE. Shocking. Took a dislike to me, he did, the first time he
   saw me.

ED. Take no notice.

SLOANE. I can't make him out.

ED. Stubborn.

SLOANE. That's why I lose my temper.

ED. I sympathize.

   Pause.

SLOANE. He deserves a good belting.

ED. You may have something there.

SLOANE. I thought you might be against me for that.

ED. No.

SLOANE. I thought you might have an exaggerated respect for the elderly.

ED. Not me.

SLOANE. I've nothing against him. (*Pause.*) But he's lived so long, he's more like an old bird than a bloke. How is it such a father has such a son? A mystery. (*Pause.*) Certainly is. (ED *pats his pockets.*) Out of fags again, are you?

ED. Yes.

SLOANE. Give them up. Never be fully fit, Ed.

ED *smiles, shakes his head.*

SLOANE. Are you going to the shop?

ED. Yes.

SLOANE. Good. (*Silence.*) How long will you be?

ED. Five minutes. Maybe ten.

SLOANE. Mmmn. (*Pause.*) Well, while you're gone I'm going to have a word with Pop.

ED. Good idea.

SLOANE. See if we can't find an area of agreement. I'll hold out the hand of friendship an' all that. I'm willing to forget the past. If he is. (*Silence.*) I'd better have a word with him. Call him.

ED. Me?

SLOANE. No good me asking him anything is there?

ED. I don't know whether we're speaking.

SLOANE. Gone funny again has he?

ED (*goes to the window, opens it, looks out. Calls*). Dad! (*Pause.*) I want a word with you.

KEMP (*off*). What's that?

Pause.

ED. Me – me – I want to see you. (*He closes the window.*) He gets worse. (*Silence.*) Appeal to his better nature. Say you're upset. Wag your finger perhaps. I don't want you to be er, well . . . at each other's throats, boy. Let's try . . . and . . . well be friends. (*Pause.*) I've the fullest confidence in your ability. (*Pause.*) Yes . . . well I'm going out now. (*Pause.*) . . . it's a funny business en it? . . . I mean . . . well, it's a ticklish problem. (*Pause.*) Yes . . . it is. (*Exit.*)

> SLOANE *sits, waits. Pause.* KEMP *enters.* SLOANE *rises, steps behind* KEMP, *bangs door.* KEMP *swings round, backs.*

KEMP. Ed? (*Pause.*) Where's Ed?

SLOANE (*takes hold of* KEMP's *stick, pulls it away from him.* KEMP *struggles.* SLOANE *wrenches stick from his hand. Leads* KEMP *to a chair*). Sit down, Pop. (KEMP *turns to go.* SLOANE *pushes him into the chair.*) Ed's not here. Gone for a walk. What you been saying about me?

KEMP. Nothing, sonnie.

SLOANE. What have you told him? What were you going to tell him?

KEMP. I – (*Pause.*) Business.

SLOANE. What kind of business? (KEMP *does not reply.*) Told him she's up the stick did you? (*No reply.*) Why did you tell him?

KEMP. He's her brother. He ought to know.

SLOANE. Fair enough.

KEMP. Got to know sometime.

SLOANE. Right. (*Silence.*) What else did you tell him? (KEMP *attempts to rise,* SLOANE *pushes him back.*) Did you say anything else? (KEMP *attempts to rise.*) Eh?

KEMP. No.

SLOANE. Were you going to?

KEMP. Yes.

SLOANE. Why?

KEMP. You're a criminal.

SLOANE. Who says I am?

KEMP. I know you are. You killed my old boss. I know it was you.

SLOANE. Your vision is faulty. You couldn't identify nobody now. So long after. You said so yourself.

KEMP. I got to go. (*Pause.*) I'm expecting delivery of a damson tree.

SLOANE. Sit still! (*Silence.*) How were you going to identify me?

KEMP. I don't have to. They got fingerprints.

SLOANE. Really?

KEMP. All over the shop.

SLOANE. It was an accident, Pop. I'm innocent. You don't know the circumstances . . .

KEMP. Oh . . . I know . . .

SLOANE. But you don't.

KEMP. You murdered him.

SLOANE. Accidental death.

Pause.

KEMP. No, sonnie . . . no.

SLOANE. You're pre-judging my case.

KEMP. You're bad.

SLOANE. I'm an orphan.

KEMP. Get away from me. Let me alone.

SLOANE (*puts the stick into* KEMP's *hand*). I trust you, Pop. Listen. Keep quiet.

Silence.

It's like this see. One day I leave the Home. Stroll along. Sky blue. Fresh air. They'd found me a likeable permanent situation. Canteen facilities. Fortnight's paid holiday. Overtime? Time and a half after midnight. A staff dance each year. What more could one wish to devote one's life to? I certainly loved that place. The air round Twickenham was like wine. Then one day I take a trip to the old man's grave. Hic Jacets in profusion. Ashes to Ashes. Alas the fleeting. The sun was declining. A few press-ups on a tomb belonging to a family name of Cavaneagh, and I left the graveyard. I thumbs a lift from a geyser who promises me a bed. Gives me a bath. And a meal. Very friendly. All you could wish he was, a photographer. He shows me one or two experimental studies. An experience for the retina and no mistake. He wanted to photo me. For certain interesting features I had that he wanted the exclusive right of preserving. You know how it is. I didn't like to refuse. No harm in it I suppose. But then I got to thinking . . . I knew a kid once called MacBride that happened to. Oh, yes . . . so when I gets to think of this I decide I got to do something about it. And I gets up in the middle of the night looking for the film see. He has a lot of expensive equipment about in his studio see. Well it appears that he gets the wrong idea. Runs in. Gives a shout. And the long and the short of it is I loses my head which is a thing I never ought to a done with the worry of them photos an all. And I hits him. I hits him.

Pause.

He must have had a weak heart. Something like that I should imagine. Definitely should have seen his doctor before that. I wasn't to know was I? I'm not to blame.

Silence.

KEMP. He was healthy. Sound as a bell.
SLOANE. How do you know?
KEMP. He won cups for it. Looked after himself.
SLOANE. A weak heart.
KEMP. Weak heart, my arse. You murdered him.
SLOANE. He fell.
KEMP. He was hit from behind.
SLOANE. I had no motive.
KEMP. The equipment.
SLOANE. I never touched it.
KEMP. You meant to.

SLOANE. Not me, Pop. (*Laughs.*) Oh, no.

KEMP. Liar . . . lying little bugger. I knew what you was from the start.

Pause.

SLOANE. What are you going to do? Are you going to tell Ed? (KEMP *makes no reply.*) He won't believe you. (KEMP *makes no reply.*) He'll think you're raving.

KEMP. No . . . you're finished. (*Attempts to rise.* SLOANE *pushes him back.* KEMP *raises his stick,* SLOANE *takes it from him.*)

SLOANE. You can't be trusted I see. I've lost faith in you. (*Throws the stick out of reach.*) Irresponsible. Can't give you offensive weapons.

KEMP. Ed will be back soon. (*Rises to go.*)

SLOANE. He will.

KEMP. I'm seeing him then.

SLOANE. Are you threatening me? Do you feel confident? Is that it? (*Stops. Clicks his tongue. Pause. Leans over and straightens* KEMP's *tie.*) Ed and me are going away. Let's have your word you'll forget it. (KEMP *does not reply.*) Pretend you never knew. Who was he? No relation. Hardly a friend. An employer. You won't bring him back by hanging me. (KEMP *does not reply.*) Where's your logic? Can I have a promise you'll keep your mouth shut?

KEMP. No.

SLOANE *twists* KEMP's *ear.*

KEMP. Ugh! aaah . . .

SLOANE. You make me desperate. I've nothing to lose, you see. One more chance, Pop. Are you going to give me away?

KEMP. I'll see the police.

SLOANE. You don't know what's good for you. (*He knocks* KEMP *behind the settee. Kicks him.*) You bring this on yourself. (*He kicks him again.*) All this could've been avoided. (KEMP `half-rises, collapses again. Pause.* SLOANE *kicks him gently with the* *toe of his boot.*) Eh, then. Wake up. (*Pause.*) Wakey, wakey. (*Silence. He goes to the door and calls.*) Ed! (*Pause.*) Ed!

KATH *comes to the door. He pushes her back.*

KATH (*off*). What's happened?
SLOANE. Where's Ed. Not you! I want Ed!

CURTAIN

ACT THREE

Door slams off.

ED (*entering*). What is it? (*Sees* KEMP *lying on the floor. Kneels.* SLOANE *enters, stands in the doorway.* KATH *tries to push past. Struggle.* SLOANE *gives up. She enters.*)

SLOANE. Some kind of attack.

ED. What did you do?

KATH. If only there were some spirits in the house. Unfortunately I don't drink myself. (*She loosens* KEMP's *collar.*) Somebody fetch his tablets.

> *Nobody moves.*

ED. He's reviving.

KATH. Speak to me, Dadda. (*Pause.*) He's been off his food for some time. (*Pause.*) He's cut his lip.

ED (*lifts* KEMP). Can you walk?

KEMP (*muttering*). Go away . . .

ED. I'll carry you upstairs. (KATH *opens the door, stands in the passage.*) He'll be better in a bit. Is his bed made?

KATH. Yes. Let him lie still and he'll get his feelings back. (ED *exits with* KEMP. *Slowly.*) Mr Sloane, did you strike the Dadda?

SLOANE. Yes.

KATH. You admit it? Did he provoke you?

SLOANE. In a way.

KATH. What a thing to do. Hit an old man. It's not like you. You're usually so gentle.

SLOANE. He upset me.

KATH. He can be aggravating I know, but you shouldn't resort to violence, dear. (*Pause.*) Did he insult you? (*Pause.*) Was it a bad word? (*Pause.*) I don't expect you can tell me what it was. I'd blush.

SLOANE. I hit him several times.

KATH. You're exaggerating. You're not that type of young man. (*Pause.*) But don't do it again. Mamma wouldn't like it. (ED *enters.*) Is he all right?

ED. Yes.

KATH. I'll go up to him.

ED. He's asleep.

KATH. Sleeping off the excitement, is he? (*Exit.*)

ED (*taking* SLOANE *aside*). How hard did you hit him?

SLOANE. Not hard.

ED. You don't know your own strength, boy. Using him like a punchbag.

SLOANE. I've told you –

ED. He's dead.

SLOANE. Dead? His heart.

ED. Whatever it was it's murder, boy. You'll have some explaining to do. (*Lights a cigarette.* KATH *enters with a carpet sweeper, begins to sweep.*)

KATH. I'd take up a toffee, but he only gets them stuck round his teeth.

ED. You're not usually at a loss, surely? You can conjure up an idea or two.

KATH. Let Mr Sloane regain his composure, Ed. Let him collect his thoughts. Forget the incident. (*She goes upstage, begins to hum 'The Indian Love Call'.*)

SLOANE *looks at* ED. ED *smiles, shakes his head.*

ED. That isn't possible, I'm afraid.

KATH. He meant no harm.

ED. What are you doing?

KATH. My housework. I mustn't neglect my chores.

ED. Can't you find a better time than this?

KATH. It's my usual time. Guess what's for dinner, Mr Sloane.

SLOANE. I'm not hungry.

ED. He doesn't want any.

KATH. Guess what mamma's prepared?

ED. Let him alone! All you think of is food. He'll be out of condition before long. As gross as you are.

KATH. Is he upset?

ED. Tell her.

SLOANE. I'm really upset.

ED. Turned your stomach, has it?

KATH. Will you feel better by this afternoon?

SLOANE. I don't know.

ED. He's worried.

KATH. The Dadda won't say anything, dear, if that's what's on your mind. He'll keep quiet. (*Pause.*) That new stove cooks excellent, Eddie.

ED. Does it?

KATH. Yes. I cooked a lovely egg yesterday. Mr Sloane had it. I think they ought to have put the grill different, though. I burned my hand.

ED. You want to look what you're doing.

KATH. It's awkwardly placed.

ED. Cooking with your eyes shut.

KATH (*pause*). You haven't guessed yet what's for dinner. Three guesses. Go on.

SLOANE. I don't know!

KATH. Chips.

SLOANE. Really?

KATH. And peas. And two eggs.

SLOANE. I don't give a sod what's for dinner!

ED. Don't use those tones to my relations, Sloane. Behave yourself for a change. (*Lights a cigarette.*)

SLOANE. Can I see you outside?

ED. What do you want to see me outside for?

SLOANE. To explain.

ED. There's nothing to explain.

SLOANE. How I came to be involved in this situation.

KATH *puts the Ewbank away.*

ED. I don't think that would be advisable. Some things will have to be sorted out. A check on your excesses is needed.

SLOANE. Are you sure he's –

ED. As forty dodos. I tried the usual methods of ascertaining; no heartbeats, no misting on my cigarette case. The finest legal brains in the country can't save you now.

KATH *re-enters.*

SLOANE. I feel sick.

KATH. It's the weather.

SLOANE. No.

KATH. Take a pill or something. I had some recommended me the other day. (*Opens a drawer, searches. She finds the tablets, shakes out two into her hand. Offers them to* SLOANE.) Take them with a glass of water. Swallow them quick. They'll relieve the symptoms.

SLOANE. I don't want them! (*He knocks them from her hand.*) I don't want pills! (*Exits.*)

KATH. He's bad, isn't he?

ED. A very bad boy.

KATH (*picks up one tablet, searches for the others, gives up*). Somebody will tread on them. That's the reason for these stains. Things get into the pile. The Dadda dropped a pickled walnut and trod it into the rug yesterday. If only we had a dog we wouldn't have so much bother.

ED. You're not having a dog.

KATH. Eddie, is Mr Sloane ill?

ED. He may be.

KATH. He looks pale. I wonder if he isn't sickening for something.

ED. He might have to go away. Something has happened which makes his presence required elsewhere.

KATH. Where?

ED. I'm not sure. Not for certain.

KATH. Is he in trouble?

ED. Dead trouble.

KATH. It was an accident, surely?

ED. You know, then?

KATH. The Dadda told me about it. Mr Sloane was unfortunate. He was joking, I expect.

ED. He never jokes.

KATH. No, he's remarkably devoid of a sense of fun. Dadda was full of it.

ED. I don't understand you.

KATH. Oh, I said he had no proof. I didn't waste my energy listening to him. Sometimes I think he makes up these things to frighten me. He ought to curb his imagination. (*Exits.*)

ED. I should have asked for references. I can see that now. The usual credentials would have avoided this. An attractive kid, so disarming, to – to tell me lies and –

KATH (*enters carrying a china figure*). This shepherdess is a lovely piece of chinawork. She comes up like new when I give her a wash.

ED. Now?

KATH. The crack spoils it, though. I should have it mended professionally. (*Exit. Re-enters carrying large vase.*) Dadda gets up to some horrible pranks lately. Throwing things into my best vase now. The habits of the elderly are beyond the pale. (*She exits. ED sits on the settee.*)

ED. I must sort out my affairs and quick.

SLOANE (*enters, glances at* ED. ED *does not look up*). Accept my apology, Ed. Sorry I was rude, but my nerves won't stand much more, I can tell you. (*He opens the suitcase. Begins to pack.*) She's got two of my shirts in the wash. Good ones. (*Opens sideboard, takes out cardigan.*) Can't risk asking her for them. (*Looks under sideboard, finds canvas shoes.*) She's been using this razor again. (*Holding up razor.*) I can tell. That's not hygienic, is it?

ED. What are you doing?

SLOANE. Packing.

ED. Why?

SLOANE. I'm going away.

ED. Where?

SLOANE. With you.

ED. No boy. Not with me.

SLOANE. It was settled.

ED. I can't allow you to take up abode in Dulverton Mansions now.

SLOANE. Why not?

ED. What a fantastic person you are. You've committed a murder!

SLOANE. An accident.

ED. Murder.

SLOANE. Those pills were undermining his constitution. Ruining his health. He couldn't have lasted much longer.

ED. Attacking a defenceless old man!

SLOANE. He had his stick.

ED. He wasn't strong enough to use it.

SLOANE. I blame that on the pills. Who prescribed them?

ED. His doctor.

SLOANE. Reputable, is he?

ED. He's on the register. What more do you want?

SLOANE. You'll find medical evidence agrees with my theory.

ED. The pills had nothing to do with it. You've no excuse. None.

SLOANE. What kind of life is it at his age?

ED. You've abused my trust.

SLOANE. I did him a service in a manner of speaking.

ED. You'll have to face the authorities.

SLOANE. Look, I'm facing no one.

ED. You've no choice.

SLOANE. I'll decide what choice I have.

ED. Get on the blower and call the law. We're finished.

SLOANE. You wouldn't put me away, would you?

ED. Without a qualm.

SLOANE. You're my friend.

ED. No friend of thugs.

SLOANE. He died of heart failure. You can't ruin my life. I'm impressionable. Think what the nick would do to me. I'd pick up criminal connexions.

ED. You already got criminal connexions.

SLOANE. Not as many as I would have.

ED. That's a point in your favour.

SLOANE. Give me a chance.

ED. You've had several.

SLOANE. One more.

ED. I've given you chances. Expected you to behave like a civilized human being.

SLOANE. Say he fell downstairs.

ED. What kind of a person does that make me?

SLOANE. A loyal friend.

ED. You'll get me six months. More than that. Depends on the judge.

SLOANE. What a legal system. Say he fell.

ED. Aiding and abetting.

SLOANE. Fake the evidence.

ED. You're completely without morals, boy. I hadn't realized how depraved you were. You murder my father. Now you ask me to help you evade Justice. Is that where my liberal principles have brought me?

SLOANE. You've got no principles.

ED. No principles? Oh, you really have upset me now. Why am I interested in your welfare? Why did I give you a job? Why do thinking men everywhere show young boys the strait and narrow? Flash cheque-books when delinquency is mentioned? Support the Scout-movement? Principles, boy, bleeding principles. And don't you dare say otherwise or you'll land in serious trouble.

SLOANE. Are you going to help me?

ED. No.

SLOANE. We must find a basis for agreement.

ED. There can be no agreement. I'm a citizen of this country. My duty is clear. You must accept responsibility for your actions.

SLOANE (*sits beside* ED. *Lays a hand on his knee*). I accept responsibility.

ED. Do you?

SLOANE. Fully.

ED. Good. Remove that hand, will you?

SLOANE. Certainly.

ED. What you just said about no principles – That's really upset me. Straight. Really upset me.

SLOANE. Sorry, Eddie, sorry.

ED. One thing I wanted to give you – my principles. Oh, I'm disillusioned. I feel I'm doing no good at all.

SLOANE. I'm very bad. Only you can help me on the road to a useful life. (*Pause.*) A couple of years ago I met a man similar to yourself. Same outlook on life. A dead ringer for you as far as physique went. He was an expert on the adolescent male body. He's completed an exhaustive study of his subject before I met him. During the course of one magical night he talked to me of his principles – offered me a job if I would accept them. Like a fool I turned him down. What an opportunity I lost, Ed. If you were to make the same demands, I'd answer loudly in the affirmative.

Pause.

ED. You mean that?

SLOANE. In future you'd have nothing to complain of.

ED. You really mean what you say?

SLOANE. Let me live with you. I'd wear my jeans out in your service. Cook for you.

ED. I eat out.

SLOANE. Bring you your tea in bed.

ED. Only women drink tea in bed.

SLOANE. You bring me my tea in bed, then. Any arrangement you fancy.

KATH *screams loudly offstage. Pause. Screams again nearer. She enters.*

KATH. Ed!

ED. Come here.

KATH. Ed, I must – (ED *takes her arm, she pulls back.*) It's Dadda – he's dead. Come quick.

ED. Sit down. (*To* SLOANE.) Bring the car round. We'll fetch the doctor.

KATH. Eddie, he's dead.

ED. I know. We know. Didn't want to upset you.

SLOANE *exits.*

KATH. I can't believe he's dead. He was in perfect health.

ED. He was ill.

KATH. Was he?

ED. You told me he was.

KATH. I didn't believe it. I only took his word for it.

ED. Didn't he say he was ill?

KATH. Often. I took no notice. You know how he is. I thought he was having me on.

ED. He was telling the truth.

KATH (*begins to sniff*). Poor Dadda. How he must have suffered. I'm truly ashamed of myself. (*She wipes her eyes on her apron.*) It's all the health scheme's fault. Will I have to send his pension book in?

ED. Yes.

KATH. I thought I would.

ED. Now listen –

KATH. Eddie.

ED. – carefully to what I say. (*He passes a hand across his mouth.*) When the doctor comes what are you going to tell him?

KATH. Me?

ED. He'll want to know.

KATH. I'll say Dadda had an attack. He passed away sudden.

ED. What about the cuts on his face?

KATH. He was rude to Mr Sloane, Eddie. Provoked him.

ED. They won't wear that.

KATH. Won't they? (*Pause.*) I shall never get in my black. I've put on weight since we buried mamma.

ED. They'll get the boy for murder.

KATH. They'd never do that would they?

ED. They'll hang him.

Pause.

KATH. Hang him?

ED. They might. I'm not sure. I get confused by the changes in the law.

KATH. Is it bad?

ED. Awful. You wouldn't see him again. You understand?

KATH. The Dadda was rude. He said a rude word about me.

ED. That's no excuse in the eyes of the law. You must say he fell downstairs.

KATH. I couldn't.

ED. I would never suggest deceiving the authorities under normal circumstances. But we have ourselves to think of. I'm in a funny position. I pay his wages. That's a tricky situation.

KATH. Is it?

ED. I'm compromised. My hands are tied. If the situation was different I might say something. Depend on it.

KATH. Wouldn't they make an exception? If we gave him a good character?

ED. He hasn't got a good character.

KATH. We could say he had.

ED. That would be perjury.

KATH. He has nice manners when he wants. I've seen them.

ED. I feel bad doing this. You see the position? He went too far. But he did it out of respect for you. That's some consideration.

KATH. He did it out of love for me?

ED. You should be grateful. No doubt of that. (*Pause.*) Do you polish that lino?

KATH. Eh?

ED. On the stairs?

KATH. No, never. I have to think of the Dadda.

ED. Go and polish them.

KATH. Doctor will be cross.

ED. Let him be.

KATH. He'll think I'm silly. He'll think I caused Dadda's fall.

ED. It doesn't matter as long as he thinks it was an accident.

KATH (*bites her lip, considers*). Shall I put Dadda's new shoes on him?

ED. Now you're using your initiative. Slippy are they?

KATH. He only wore them once.

ED. Good girl.

> SLOANE *enters*.

SLOANE. Ready? Come on, then.

> ED *nods to* KATH, *waiting. She looks from one to the other. Notices the case.*

KATH. Why is he taking his case?

ED. He's coming with me. He can't stay here.

KATH. Why not?

ED. They'll suspect.

> *Pause.*

KATH. When is he coming back?

ED. Day after next.

KATH. He doesn't need that big case. (*She exits.*)

ED. Get in the car, boy.

SLOANE. How about my shirts?

ED. I'll see about buying a couple.

KATH (*off*). Why is he taking his clothes?

ED. What are you on about?

KATH *returns*.

KATH. I've just checked. They aren't in the laundry basket.

ED. Snooping around. Don't you trust me?

KATH. You're taking him away.

SLOANE. We thought I ought to live in.

KATH. Do you want to leave?

SLOANE. I'll be back when this has blown over.

KATH. Why are you leaving your mamma? There's no need for him to go away, Eddie. Doctor knows he lives here.

ED. He'll instigate proceedings.

KATH. Doctors don't do that. He wants to stay.

ED. Ask him. (*To* SLOANE.) Do you want to stay?

SLOANE. No.

ED. The question is answered.

KATH. Ed –

ED. Send a wire –

KATH. I've something to tell you.

She lifts her apron. Shyly.

I've a bun in the oven.

ED. You've a whole bloody baker's shop in the oven from the look of that.

KATH. Mr Sloane was nice to me. Aren't you shocked?

ED. No, it's what I expect of you.

KATH. Aren't you angry with Mr Sloane?

ED. I'm angry with you.

KATH. Are you?

ED. Mr Sloane's already explained.

KATH. What did he explain?

ED. How you carried on.

KATH. I didn't carry on! What a wicked thing to say.

ED. Seducing him.

KATH. Did he say that?

ED. Told me the grisly details.

Silence.

KATH. Mr Sloane, dear, take back your locket.

ED. What locket?

KATH. He gave me a locket. (*She takes off the locket.* SLOANE *attempts to take it.*) I don't believe he'd take it if you weren't here, Ed. (*She puts the locket back. To* SLOANE.) How could you behave so bad. Accusing me of seducing you.

SLOANE. But you did!

KATH. That's neither here nor there. Using expressions like that. Making yourself cheap. (SLOANE *turns to the suitcase.*) I see the truth of the matter. He's been at you. Isn't that like him?

ED. He wants to come with me.

KATH. Let him decide for himself.

ED. He's got problems. Needs a man's hand on his shoulder.

KATH. I'm afraid you're unduly influencing him.

ED. You've been found out.

KATH. Found out?

ED. Exposed.

KATH. Rubbish!

ED. Making a spectacle of yourself. Corrupting a kid young enough to be your son.

KATH. He loves me.

ED. Prove it.

KATH. A woman knows when she's loved.

ED. I blame myself for letting him stay. Knowing your character.

KATH. My character will stand analysis.

ED. You're older than him.

KATH. I'm a benign influence. A source of good.

ED. You spoil him.

KATH. Who tucks him up at night? And he likes my cooking. He won't deny that.

ED. No.

KATH. See I'm right.

ED. I can't argue with you.

KATH. You can't.

ED. You don't make sense.

KATH. I do.

ED. You have no logical train of thought.

KATH. What is that?

ED. No power of argument.

KATH. I keep his trousers pressed nice. He's been smarter since I knew him.

ED. He's lost with you.

KATH. I gave him everything.

ED. No backbone. Spineless.

KATH. He's lovely with me. Charming little baby he is.

ED. No, he's soft. You softened him up.

KATH. I gave him three meals a day. Porridge for breakfast. Meat and two veg for dinner. A fry for tea. And cheese for supper. What more could he want?

ED. Freedom.

KATH. He's free with me.

ED. You're immoral.

KATH. It's natural.

ED. He's clean-living by nature; that's every man's right.

KATH. What are you going to give him?

ED. The world.

KATH (*comes round the case, looks in*). The state of this case. Mr Sloane, dear, you can't even pack. See how he needs me in the smallest things? Can't manage without a woman.

ED. Let him try.

KATH. Women are necessary.

ED. Granted.

KATH. Where's your argument?

ED. In limited doses.

KATH. You're silly, Eddie, silly . . .

ED. Let him choose. Let's have it in black and white, boy.

SLOANE. I'm going with Ed.

ED *nods, smacks* SLOANE's *shoulder, laughs.*

KATH. Is it the colour of the curtains in your room?

SLOANE. No.

KATH. Is it because I'm pregnant?

SLOANE. No. Better opportunities. A new life.

KATH. You vowed you loved me.

SLOANE. Never for a second.

KATH. I was kind to you.

SLOANE. Yes.

KATH. Are you grateful?

SLOANE. I paid.

KATH. I paid too. Baby on the way. Reputation ruined.

SLOANE. You had no reputation.

KATH. Is that what he's taught you?

ED. I taught him nothing. He was innocent until you got your maulers on to him.

KATH. He'd packed the experience of a lifetime into a few short years.

ED. Pure in heart, he was. He wouldn't know where to put it.

KATH. I attracted him instantly.

ED. You couldn't attract a blind man.

KATH. He wanted to marry me.

ED. What a bride!

KATH. We were to ask your consent.

ED. Look in the glass, lady. Let's enjoy a laugh. (*He takes her to the mirror.*) What do you see?

KATH. Me.

ED. What are you?

KATH. My hair is nice. Natural. I'm mature, but still able to command a certain appeal.

ED. You look like death!

She shakes him off. He drags her back to the mirror.

ED. Flabby mouth. Wrinkled neck. Puffy hands.

KATH. It's baby coming.

ED. Sagging tits. You cradle-snatcher.

KATH. He said I was a Venus. I held him in my arms.

ED. What a martyrdom!

KATH. He wanted for nothing. I loved him sincerely.

ED. You're appetite appalled him.

KATH. I loved him.

ED. Insatiable.

KATH (*to* SLOANE). Baby, my little boy . . .

ED. He aches at every organ.

KATH. . . . mamma forgives you.

ED. What have you to offer? You're fat and the crows-feet under your eyes would make you an object of terror. Pack it in, I tell you. Sawdust up to the navel? You've nothing to lure any man.

KATH. Is that the truth, Mr Sloane?

SLOANE. More or less.

KATH. Why didn't you tell me?

ED. How could he tell you? You showed him the gate of Hell every night. He abandoned Hope when he entered there.

KATH (*snaps the suitcase shut*). Mr Sloane, I believed you were a good boy. I find you've deceived me.

SLOANE. You deceived yourself.

KATH. Perhaps. (*She holds out her hand.*) Kiss my hand, dear, in the manner of the theatre. (*He kisses her hand.*) I shall cry. (*She feels for a handkerchief.*)

ED. On with the waterworks.

KATH. I'm losing you for ever.

SLOANE. I'll pop round.

KATH. I'll not be able to bear it.

SLOANE. You'll have the baby.

KATH. I shall die of it, I'm sure.

ED. What a cruel performance you're giving. Like an old tart grinding to her climax.

SLOANE *kisses* KATH's *cheek.*

KATH. Baby . . . (*She holds him close. Looks at* ED *over* SLOANE's *shoulder.*) Before you go, Mr Sloane, we must straighten things out. The Dadda's death was a blow to me.

SLOANE (*releases her*). Ed can vouch for me. You can support his story.

KATH. What story?

SLOANE. The old man fell downstairs.

KATH. I shall never under any circumstances allow anyone to perjure me. It was murder.

Pause. SLOANE *releases her. Pause.*

SLOANE. He was ill.

KATH. Ah, you know as well as I he was perfectly healthy this morning.

SLOANE. Ed will give me an alibi.

KATH. He wasn't there, dear. Respect the truth always. It's the least you can do under the circumstances.

SLOANE. He'll say he was a witness.

KATH. It's not in accordance with my ideas of morality.

SLOANE. Look – mamma . . . see –

KATH. When doctor comes he'll want to know things. Are you asking me to deceive our G.P.? He's an extremely able man. He'll notice discrepancies. And then where will we be? He'd make his report and mamma would be behind bars. I'm sure that isn't your idea. Is it?

SLOANE. Ed is supporting me.

KATH. He must decide for himself. I won't practise a falsehood.

SLOANE. You're not going back on your word?

KATH. You know how I go to pieces under cross-examination.

SLOANE. Make an effort.

KATH. Who for?

SLOANE. Me.

KATH. You won't be here.

SLOANE. I'll come and see you.

KATH. No. Call me names if you wish, but I won't tell stories. I'm a firm believer in truth.

ED. Look . . . Kathy – Say you were out when the accident occurred.

KATH. No.

ED. Down the shops.

KATH. But I wasn't.

ED. You didn't see him fall.

KATH. I would have heard him.

ED. Say you were out of range.

KATH. No.

ED. Forget the whole business.

KATH. No.

ED. Go to the police then. What will you achieve? Nothing. This boy was carried away by the exuberance of youth. He's under age.

KATH (*hands the suitcase to* ED). You struck the Dadda down in cold blood, Mr Sloane. In the course of conversations before his death he told me one or two things of interest.

SLOANE. Concerning whom?

KATH. We talked only of you. I could hardly give credence to the report of your crimes. I didn't believe the old man. I'm paid for it now.

ED. The last word, eh? Using your whore's prerogative?

KATH. Stay with me.

SLOANE. No.

KATH. Hold me tight again.

SLOANE. No.

KATH. There's no need to go away, dear. Don't make me unhappy.

SLOANE. I'm going with Ed.

KATH. I was never subtle, Mr Sloane . . . If you go with Eddie, I'll tell the police.

SLOANE. If I stay here he'll do the same.

ED. It's what is called a dilemma, boy. You are on the horns of it.

   Silence.

KATH. You see how things are, Mr Sloane?

SLOANE *smacks her face, she screams.*

ED. What are you doing?

SLOANE. Leave her to me.

KATH. Don't attempt to threaten me.

ED. There's no suggestion of threats.

KATH. What's he doing then?

ED. Let her alone, boy.

SLOANE. Keep out of this! (ED *lays a hand on* SLOANE's *shoulder, tries to pull him away from* KATH. SLOANE *turns, shoves* ED *from him.*) Did you hear what I said? Keep out of it!

ED. Don't be violent. No violence at any cost. (SLOANE *gets* KATH *into a corner; struggles with her.*) What's this exhibition for? This is gratuitous violence. Give over, both of you!

SLOANE (*shakes* KATH). Support me, you mare! Support me!

KATH. Make him stop! I shall be sick. He's upsetting my insides.

ED (*runs round*). What did you want to provoke him for?

SLOANE *shakes* KATH *harder.* She screams.

KATH. My teeth! (*She claps a hand over her mouth.*) My teeth. (SLOANE *flings her from him. She crawls round the floor, searching.*) He's broke my teeth! Where are they?

ED. Expensive equipment gone west now see? I'm annoyed with you, boy. Seriously annoyed. Giving us the benefit of your pauperism. Is this what we listen to the Week's Good Cause for? A lot of vicars and actresses making appeals for cash gifts to raise hooligans who can't control themselves? I'd've given my cheque to the anti-Jewish League if I'd known.

KATH (*reaching under the settee*). I'll still forgive and forget.

ED. Coming in here as a lodger. Raised in a charity home. The lack of common courtesy in some people is appalling.

SLOANE. She's won! The bitch has won!

He grips ED's arm. ED shrugs him away.

ED. We'll discuss the matter.

SLOANE. We need action not discussion. Persuade her. Cut her throat, but persuade her!

ED. Don't use that tone of voice to me, boy. I won't be dictated to. (*Pause.*) Perhaps we can share you.

SLOANE. Deal with her.

ED. We'll think of something.

SLOANE. She must be primed. Get her evidence correct.

ED. Don't worry. I'm in perfect control of the situation.

SLOANE. You're in control of nothing! Where are your influential friends? Ring them, we need protection.

KATH. It's his nerves. He doesn't know what he's doing.

ED. Put your teeth in, will you? Sitting there with them in your hand.

KATH. He's broke them.

ED. They're only chipped. Go on, turn your back.

KATH (*puts her teeth in*). What are we going to do, Eddie?

ED. Stand up. We can't conduct a serious discussion from that position.

KATH. Help me up, Mr Sloane. Thank you, baby. See, Ed, he hasn't lost respect for me.

ED. An arrangement to suit all tastes. That is what's needed.

KATH. I don't want to lose my baby.

ED. You won't lose him.

KATH. But –

ED. (*holds up a hand*). What are your main requirements? I take it there's no question of making an honest woman of you? You don't demand the supreme sacrifice?

SLOANE. I'm not marrying her!

ED. Calm down will you?

SLOANE. Remember our agreement

ED. I'm keeping it in mind, boy.

SLOANE. Don't saddle me with her for life.

KATH. He's close to tears. Isn't he sweet?

ED. Yes, he's definitely attractive in adversity. Really, boy, what with one thing and another . . . I warned you against women, didn't I? They land you in impossible predicaments of this nature.

SLOANE. You can solve it, Ed.

ED. You believe that, do you? I hope so. Marriage is a non-starter, then?

KATH. He's led me on.

ED. Are you repentant now? Truly ashamed of yourself?

SLOANE. I am.

ED. You aren't going to press your claims are you? Even if he thee worshipped with his body, his mind would be elsewhere. And a wife cannot testify against her husband.

KATH. Can't she?

ED. No, a minor point.

KATH. I don't mind about marriage as long as he doesn't leave me.

ED. Fine. (*Pause.*) I think, boy, you'd better go and wait in the car. Keep the engine running. I won't be long. I want a private talk with my sister.

SLOANE. Is it going to be O.K.?

ED. Well . . . perhaps.

SLOANE. I'll be grateful.

ED. Will you?

SLOANE. Eternally.

ED. Not eternally, boy. Just a few years (*He pats* SLOANE *on the shoulder.* SLOANE *exits.*) What will the story be?

KATH. Like you said – he fell downstairs.

ED. That will explain the cuts and bruises. You'd better say you were out. Stick to that. You know nothing. I'll manage the doctor.

KATH. Yes, Ed.

ED. Can I trust you?

KATH. Yes.

ED. Then let's have no more threats. You'll support him?

KATH. As long as he stays here.

ED. You've had him six months; I'll have him the next six. I'm not robbing you of him permanently.

KATH. Aren't you?

ED. No question of it. (*Pause.*) As long as you're prepared to accept the idea of partnership.

KATH. For how long?

ED. As long as the agreement lasts.

KATH. How long is that?

ED. By the half-year.

KATH. That's too long, dear. I get so lonely.

ED. I've got no objections if he visits you from time to time. Briefly. We could put it in the contract. Fair enough?

KATH. Yes.

ED. I'd bring him over myself in the car. Now, you'll be more or less out of action for the next three months. So shall we say till next August? Agreed?

KATH. Perfect, Eddie. It's very clever of you to have thought of such a lovely idea!

ED. Put it down to my experience at the conference table.

Car sounds off.

KATH. Can he be present at the birth of his child?

ED. You're not turning him into a mid-wife.

KATH. It deepens the relationship if the father is there.

ED. It's all any reasonable child can expect if the dad is present at the conception. Let's hear no more of it. Give me that locket.

KATH. It was his present to me.

ED. You'll get it back in March. (*She hands him the locket. He puts it on.*) And behave yourself in future. I'm not having you pregnant every year. I'll have a word with him about it. (*He kisses her cheek, pats her bottom.*) Be a good girl.

KATH. Yes, Ed.

ED. Well, it's been a pleasant morning. See you later. (*He exits. The front door slams.* KATH *goes to the sideboard and rummages in drawer; takes out a sweet, unwraps it and puts it into her mouth. Sits on settee.*)

CURTAIN

Methuen Modern Plays

include work by

Jean Anouilh
John Arden
Margaretta D'Arcy
Peter Barnes
Sebastian Barry
Brendan Behan
Dermot Bolger
Edward Bond
Bertolt Brecht
Howard Brenton
Anthony Burgess
Simon Burke
Jim Cartwright
Caryl Churchill
Noël Coward
Lucinda Coxon
Sarah Daniels
Nick Darke
Nick Dear
Shelagh Delaney
David Edgar
David Eldridge
Dario Fo
Michael Frayn
John Godber
Paul Godfrey
David Greig
John Guare
Peter Handke
David Harrower
Jonathan Harvey
Iain Heggie
Declan Hughes
Terry Johnson
Sarah Kane
Charlotte Keatley
Barrie Keeffe
Howard Korder

Robert Lepage
Stephen Lowe
Doug Lucie
Martin McDonagh
John McGrath
Terrence McNally
David Mamet
Patrick Marber
Arthur Miller
Mtwa, Ngema & Simon
Tom Murphy
Phyllis Nagy
Peter Nichols
Joseph O'Connor
Joe Orton
Louise Page
Joe Penhall
Luigi Pirandello
Stephen Poliakoff
Franca Rame
Mark Ravenhill
Philip Ridley
Reginald Rose
David Rudkin
Willy Russell
Jean-Paul Sartre
Sam Shepard
Wole Soyinka
Shelagh Stephenson
C. P. Taylor
Theatre de Complicite
Theatre Workshop
Sue Townsend
Judy Upton
Timberlake Wertenbaker
Roy Williams
Victoria Wood

Methuen World Classics

include

Jean Anouilh (two volumes)
John Arden (two volumes)
Arden & D'Arcy
Brendan Behan
Aphra Behn
Bertolt Brecht (six volumes)
Büchner
Bulgakov
Calderón
Čapek
Anton Chekhov
Noël Coward (seven volumes)
Eduardo De Filippo
Max Frisch
John Galsworthy
Gogol
Gorky
Harley Granville Barker
   (two volumes)
Henrik Ibsen (six volumes)
Lorca (three volumes)

Marivaux
Mustapha Matura
David Mercer (two volumes)
Arthur Miller (five volumes)
Molière
Musset
Peter Nichols (two volumes)
Clifford Odets
Joe Orton
A. W. Pinero
Luigi Pirandello
Terence Rattigan
   (two volumes)
W. Somerset Maughan
   (two volumes)
August Strindberg
   (three volumes)
J. M. Synge
Ramón del Valle-Inclán
Frank Wedekind
Oscar Wilde

Methuen Student Editions

Methuen Classical Greek Dramatists

Aeschylus Plays: One
(Persians, Seven against Thebes, Suppliants,
Prometheus Bound)

Aeschylus Plays: Two
(Oresteia: Agamemnon, Libation-Bearers, Eumenides)

Aristophanes Plays: One
(Acharnians, Knights, Peace, Lysistrata)

Aristophanes Plays: Two
(Wasps, Clouds, Birds, Festival Time, Frogs)

Aristophanes & Menander: New Comedy
(Women in Power, Wealth, The Malcontent,
The Woman from Samos)

Euripides Plays: One
(Medea, The Phoenician Women, Bacchae)

Euripides Plays: Two
(Hecuba, The Women of Troy, Iphigenia at Aulis,
Cyclops)

Euripides Plays: Three
(Alkestis, Helen, Ion)

Euripides Plays: Four
(Elektra, Orestes, Iphigeneia in Tauris)

Euripides Plays: Five
(Andromache, Herakles' Children, Herakles)

Euripides Plays: Six
(Hippolytos, Suppliants, Rhesos)

Sophocles Plays: One (The Theban Plays)
(Oedipus the King, Oedipus at Colonus, Antigone)

Sophocles Plays: Two
(Ajax, Women of Trachis, Electra, Philoctetes)

A SELECTED LIST OF
METHUEN MODERN PLAYS

☐ CLOSER	Patrick Marber	£6.99
☐ THE BEAUTY OF QUEEN OF LEENANE	Martin McDonagh	£6.99
☐ A SKULL IN CONNEMARA	Martin McDonagh	£6.99
☐ THE LONESOME WEST	Martin McDonagh	£6.99
☐ THE CRIPPLE OF INISHMAAN	Martin McDonagh	£6.99
☐ THE STEWARD OF CHRISTENDOM	Sebastian Barry	£6.99
☐ SHOPPING AND F***ING	Mark Ravenhill	£6.99
☐ FAUST (FAUST IS DEAD)	Mark Ravenhill	£5.99
☐ COPENHAGEN	Michael Frayn	£6.99
☐ POLYGRAPH	Robert Lepage and Marie Brasssard	£6.99
☐ BEAUTIFUL THING	Jonathan Harvey	£6.99
☐ MEMORY OF WATER & FIVE KINDS OF SILENCE	Shelagh Stephenson	£7.99
☐ WISHBONES	Lucinda Coxon	£6.99
☐ BONDAGES & THE STRAW CHAIR	Sue Glover	£9.99
☐ SOME VOICES & PALE HORSE	Joe Penhall	£7.99
☐ KNIVES IN HENS	David Harrower	£6.99
☐ BOYS LIFE & SEARCH AND DESTROY	Howard Korder	£8.99
☐ THE LIGHTS	Howard Korder	£6.99
☐ SERVING IT UP & A WEEK WITH TONY	David Eldridge	£8.99
☐ INSIDE TRADING	Malcolm Bradbury	£6.99
☐ MASTERCLASS	Terence McNally	£5.99
☐ EUROPE & THE ARCHITECT	David Grieg	£7.99
☐ BLUE MURDER	Peter Nichols	£6.99
☐ BLASTED & PHAEDRA'S LOVE	Sarah Kane	£7.99

METHUEN STUDENT EDITIONS

* All Methuen Drama books are available through mail order or from your local bookshop, or online at www.methuen.co.uk.

Please send cheque/eurocheque/postal order (sterling only) Access, Visa, Mastercard, Diners Card, Switch or Amex.

Expiry Date: .... Signature: ....

Please allow 75 pence per book for post and packing U.K.

Overseas customers please allow £1.00 per copy for post and packing.

ALL ORDERS TO:

Methuen Books, Books by Post, TBS Limited, The Book Service, Colchester Road, Frating Green, Colchester, Essex CO7 7DW.

NAME: ....

ADDRESS: ....

....

....

Please allow 28 days for delivery. Please tick box if you do not wish to receive any additional information ☐

Prices and availability subject to change without notice.

For a complete catalogue of Methuen Drama titles
write to:

Methuen Drama
215 Vauxhall Bridge Road
London SW1V 1EJ

or you can visit our website at:

www.methuen.co.uk